LITERACY AND LABELS:

*A Look at Literacy Policy and
People With a Mental Handicap*

THE G. ALLAN ROEHER INSTITUTE

Copyright © 1990, The G. Allan Roeher Institute

Canadian Cataloguing in Publication Data

The G. Allan Roeher Institute
  Literacy and labels: a look at literacy policy and people with
  a mental handicap

ISBN 0-920121-46-2

Issued also in French under the title: Etiquette et alphabet:
  un regard sur la question des politiques d'alphabétisation
  et la personne qui présente un handicap intellectual.

1. Literacy. 2. Mentally handicapped - Education.
I. G. Allan Roeher Institute

LC149.I57 1990   371.92'80444   C90-095051-X

The G. Allan Roeher Institute
4700 Keele Street, Kinsmen Building, York University,
Downsview, Ontario, Canada M3J 1P3 (416) 661-9611

Institute Director:	Marcia Rioux
Researcher-Author:	Michael Bach
Editors:	Wanda Taylor
	Giovanna Heffernan
Desktop Publishing:	Victor Salus

The G. Allan Roeher Institute

Canada's National Institute for the Study of Public Policy Affecting Persons with an Intellectual Impairment

The G. Allan Roeher Institute has two major goals:

• to identify and anticipate future trends that will support the presence, participation, self-determination and contribution of persons with an intellectual impairment in their communities;

• to foster the exchange of ideas leading to new ways of thinking about persons with an intellectual impairment.

The Institute conducts, sponsors and publishes research in a wide range of areas, with a major focus on public policy and funding, on studies of innovative social programs and on the development of policy alternatives. It offers training programs and workshops across Canada on topics such as integrated education, post secondary education, leisure, employment, and alternatives to intrusive methods of behaviour modification. Through its Information Services, which include a library, a book and film distribution service, and a computer accessible information system, The Institute provides up-to-date information to the public, professionals and community groups. The Institute also publishes the quarterly magazine **entourage**.

The G. Allan Roeher Institute is sponsored by the Canadian Association for Community Living, a voluntary organization bringing together over 400 local and twelve provincial and territorial associations working on behalf of persons with an intellectual impairment.

For more information about The G. Allan Roeher Institute, please contact us at:

4700 Keele Street, Kinsmen Building, York University, Downsview, Ontario, Canada M3J 1P3 (416) 661-9611

CONTENTS

FOREWORD

FOREWORD

Education has, for at least the past century, been a major concern of Western nations. Compulsory education of children has been, for many years, a cornerstone of Canadian social policy. Governments invest billions of dollars every year to ensure that citizens have, at least, a basic education within a universally available, publicly financed education system. This investment is important because it provides the individual with the skills necessary to exercise citizenship, and to participate in the social and cultural life of our society. It also ensures that the needed labour market skills are available to maintain an economic and social standard that is the goal of government.

In the past decade, however, it has become evident that there are many people who, despite this investment of political will and funds, are not in fact literate. This fact has come perhaps as less of a surprise to those who work within the mental handicap movement than to others. Only since the 1940s in Canada has there been any concern about the education of those labelled mentally handicapped. It was parents of those labelled individuals who first organized schools to ensure that their children had access to any education at all. And it was not until the 1950s that governments took over the financial responsibility for providing education, albeit in segregated schools or classes according to their classification as "trainable" or "educable" — categories which, unfortunately, are still in common use today.

In an attempt to examine how persons with mental handicaps live in Canada today and in line with the rights guaranteed by the Canadian *Charter of Rights and Freedoms*, The G. Allan Roeher Institute has undertaken this study as part of its overall research and policy development program. The United Nations has declared 1990 to be the International Literacy Year, a year to focus on the unacceptably high levels of illiteracy despite conscious attempts to combat illiteracy. In the hoopla that has surrounded the year little has been said about those who have a mental handicap. Where they fit into the equation, what programs are accessible to them, how they can access literacy skills, what rights they have to a basic education, have all but been ignored. This also does not come as a surprise to many people with a mental handicap or to those who struggle for social change on their behalf. When asked, those with a mental handicap will tell you that they are tired of hearing that they cannot learn, that they are unproductive, that their rights are limited by their handicap. But they know that that is the general perception of the public and of governments who establish and finance literacy and education programs. They also know that it is not true. They are illiterate because there has been no systematic attempt to recognize their skills and their abilities, that is, to include them in the basic education that so many take for granted. They will also tell you that they are fed up with being ignored and with being unable to participate as full and contributing members of society. They don't want charity, they don't want to live on government handouts, they don't want to be handicapped by their illiteracy and by the general lack of interest that has been manifested by the public and the federal, provincial and territorial governments to their lack of literacy.

If there is to be a solution to the problem of illiteracy in Canada, then those with a mental handicap must also be included in the policy making that surrounds the issue. Any individual who is illiterate has a legitimate claim to access to the services that address that problem. That inevitably includes the development of new approaches to teaching and learning in cases where populations who have conventionally not been included are included. It is not acceptable or just to exclude people because we do not yet know how to instruct. Services must be tailored to the needs of those who need them. For too long, individuals have had to qualify to fit within the parameters of the services and for those with a mental handicap this has been their handicap. It is, in other words, the service that is lacking not the individual. While this may sound and indeed probably is somewhat radical, it is only once we recognize the inadequacies of the service and funding structures, that we can begin to develop approaches that will resolve the issues. The time is ripe to start recognizing the weaknesses in the system and to move to correct the inadequacies.

There are a number of people I would like to thank for the contribution to this study. First, I want to acknowledge the Literacy Program in the Department of the Secretary of State for the financing of this study and for their recognition that it is important to take into account the real problem of illiteracy for people with a mental handicap.

Second, I would like to thank Michael Bach who was the principal author and researcher on this study. As well I would like to thank others who carried out interviews and reviewed documents for this study: Anne George in British Columbia and Lorraine Bonneville in Quebec. Skip McCarthy provided invaluable assistance in analyzing the data from the Health and Activity Limitation Survey. I would also like to recognize the significant contribution of those who worked on and reviewed drafts of the study including Cameron Crawford, Wanda Taylor, Giovanna Heffernan, Diane Richler, and Joan Macintosh.

Third, I appreciate the time and effort of government officials and people within the literacy movement who provided the information on which the study was based. Literally dozens of people were approached for information or for interviews and each of these people gave freely of their time and knowledge.

Finally, I would like to most sincerely thank the people within the community living movement and in particular those self-advocates who provided us with the poignant stories and insights that make up the core of this work. I can only hope that this report will be widely distributed, read and acted upon to enable all individuals to learn the literacy skills they need or want to participate as citizens in Canadian society.

Marcia H. Rioux
Director

INTRODUCTION

There is a problem, some say a "crisis" of low levels of literacy among adults. The problem has been related to such factors as limited access to basic education for large proportions of the world's population; technological changes that require ever-new literacy skills; the increasing value placed on the ability of individuals to manage and process large amounts of print information; and the need for literacy skills if individuals are to fully enjoy their legal and citizenship rights. Spurred in part by the United Nations declaration of 1990 as International Literacy Year, the problem of low levels of literacy has become the theme of numerous studies, books, conferences, and governmental task forces. Reports, research, and policy statements have sought to define the scope and scale of the problem, and to specify its remedies.

The research during the past number of years has defined some groups as being particulary vulnerable to "illiteracy" - immigrant populations, prison populations, native populations, the poor, rural populations, etc. Conspicuously absent from the research and from policy statements, however, is reference to literacy as an issue for adults with a mental handicap. This report addresses that absence in current research and in policy and program development. It examines the kinds of barriers faced by those with a mental handicap in gaining access to literacy education. It also considers the kinds of policy and program supports that are required to enable greater participation.

Because there is very little research or literature that examines the relationship between literacy and mental handicap, this study has been exploratory in nature. Issues of literacy and mental handicap were identified through an overview of literature in the field of literacy and in the field of mental handicap. The study included an analysis of the data base of the *Health and Activity*

Limitation Survey (HALS) in order to examine levels of literacy, labour force status, and poverty among adults with a mental handicap. There were 2,948 adults clearly identified in HALS as having a mental handicap. This was the sample used in carrying out the statistical analysis for this study. However, this number is, in all likelihood, well below the number of people who should have been identifiable within the Survey as having a mental handicap. A greater number of individuals were not identifiable for reasons related to the design of the Survey. While it must be acknowledged that the statistics presented in this study should be regarded with caution it must also be pointed out that the number of individuals identified is significant, and that the statistical analysis yields important insight into the issues under investigation.

As well, telephone and face-to-face interviews were held with self-advocates who have been involved in literacy education, representatives of provincial Associations for Community Living, a representative from National People First, government officials responsible for literacy funding, programs, and coordination, program coordinators, and literacy educators. Individuals from each province and territory were interviewed for the study.

Chapter 1 examines different approaches to defining literacy and considers the relevance of these approaches to adults with a mental handicap. Chapter 2 examines issues that arise in measuring levels of literacy among adults with a mental handicap, and provides estimates of the level of literacy among adults labelled in this way. Chapter 3 examines the scope of the problem of literacy. It identifies common themes from the literature about the need for literacy and considers implications for adults with a mental handicap. It is in the context of a growing recognition of the scope and the scale of the literacy problem that Chapter 4 looks at the relationship between literacy, learning, and mental handicap. Some common assumptions about this relationship are examined. Chapter 5 provides an overview of the framework for delivery of literacy education in Canada. Chapter 6 examines barriers to literacy education for adults with a mental handicap. Chapter 7 looks at proposals for literacy policy in Canada. The final chapter provides a summary of conclusions drawn in this study and makes recommendations for policy development and the delivery of literacy education. An Appendix provides a contact list of provincial/territorial literacy organizations, of provincial/territorial Associations for Community Living, and of National People First.

CHAPTER 1

DEFINING LITERACY

Defining the meaning of the term "literacy" is the subject of much debate. There exists a large literature on literacy that includes many ways of defining the concept. How literacy is defined, and how problems that result from low levels of literacy are framed, shape the kinds of policies, programs, and materials that are developed to address the problems. Literacy is defined in three ways in this report: *basic* literacy, *functional* literacy, and *critical* literacy.

Basic literacy refers to the acquisition of rudimentary reading, writing and numeracy skills. Functional literacy usually refers to the ability to use reading, writing, and numeracy skills to achieve one's own goals and to participate in the social and economic life of the community. Critical literacy refers to the acquisition by individuals and groups who have been marginalized in society, of the means to communicate their experience and interests in public discourse.

The approaches to literacy education informed by these definitions are not mutually exclusive. Many literacy programs encompass aspects of all three definitions, though they may vary in their emphasis.

BASIC LITERACY

Basic literacy refers to the basic and rudimentary skills of reading, writing and numeracy. A person without basic literacy was defined in a 1978 UNESCO document as one who could not "with understanding both read and write a short simple statement on his [sic] everyday life".[1] However, even basic literacy skills are often considered inadequate to function in a world where technological change is rapid, where individuals encounter increasing amounts of print information in their everyday life, and where the demands of the workplace often require that individuals continually adapt and acquire new skills. With respect to individuals with some form of intellectual or learning disability, Patton and Polloway suggest that programs that include an emphasis on development of basic reading and academic skills are necessary. However, they caution that programs designed exclusively for remediation or development of basic skills tend to be "deficit-oriented, focusing on student weaknesses," and that they may be inappropriate to the demands of adulthood.[2]

FUNCTIONAL LITERACY

Functional literacy is generally seen as the ability to apply the skills of basic literacy to one's social, community, and working environment as one wishes and as these skills are required. This definition has informed educational policies and literacy programs. The purpose of such policies and programs is to assist adults in acquiring the literacy skills necessary for employment, for carrying out activities of daily life, and for participating in the civic and political institutions of society.

Most of the literature on literacy has defined the essence of the problem as one of low levels of functional literacy in the population. One of the first and most influential formulations of this concept appeared in 1956 in a UNESCO document written by William S. Gray. He defined a person as functionally literate when he or she:

> has acquired the knowledge and skills in reading and writing which enable him [sic] to engage in all those activities in which literacy is normally assumed in his [sic] culture or group.[3]

Throughout the 1970s and 1980s increasing the rate of functional literacy among the population was seen by governments as a key to furthering global economic development, and as a necessary response to the current and anticipated demand for skilled labour. Forecasts on the demand for skilled labour emphasize a declining proportion of youth in the population.[4] A decline in the size of the productive labour force is happening at a time when the demands of the workplace are changing through the introduction of new technologies, through a decline in the number of jobs in the manufacturing sector, and an increase in the number of administrative, technical, and service jobs. Literacy itself is being redefined by such changes, especially changes in technology.

While assumptions about a "causal" relationship between functional literacy and economic prosperity have not gone unchallenged[5], this thinking has influenced development strategies in different countries including Canada. For example, the 1985 Education Report of the Newfoundland Royal Commission on Employment and Unemployment stated: "Literacy is a prerequisite for modern-day economic development. Without it scientific, technological and other advances cannot be obtained and the economy cannot achieve self-sustained growth."[6]

That there is a substantial economic and social cost to low levels of functional literacy has also been argued by analysts in the literacy field. Kozol has estimated that 60 million people in the United States are functionally illiterate, and that the cost to the American economy and society is in excess of $20 billion.[7] The Canadian Business Task Force on Literacy has estimated the cost of illiteracy to business in Canada to be $4 billion annually and to society in general to be $10 billion annually. Cost factors used included lost earnings from unemployment, direct training expenditures, unemployment insurance expenditures, 10 percent of federal expenditures on correctional facilities (a high percentage of those in federal prisons are expected to have low levels of literacy), and the cost of industrial accidents.[8] As the study indicates, the extent to which such cost factors can be directly related to levels of literacy is open to some question.

In the 1970s literacy began to emerge as a human rights issue and functional literacy was formulated in terms even broader than those outlined by Gray twenty years earlier. Hunter and Harman provided a definition of literacy in 1979 that

6

has guided much of the thinking since. Their emphasis on both individual self-determination and "functional" participation in the community are now recurring features of the definition of literacy in policy statements and program objectives. They defined functional literacy as:

> the possession of skills perceived as necessary by particular persons and groups to fulfill their own self-determined objectives as family and community members, citizens, consumers, job holders, and members of social, religious or other associations of their choosing.[9]

This contemporary definition of functional literacy recognizes a diversity in the ends to which literacy will be put by any one individual or group, and the demands that will be placed upon them. Functional literacy is, then, highly "situational." The demand for literacy skills depends both on the goals of the individual, and the requirements imposed by technologies, the nature of work, and the print information encountered in daily life.

CRITICAL LITERACY

The concept of critical literacy has emerged through the work of adult educators with those who are socially or economically marginalized. Paulo Freire, through his work with such groups in Latin America, is commonly associated with the development of this approach.[10] There is now a growing theory and practice in the area of critical literacy.[11] A critical literacy perspective challenges assumptions about: (1) the relationship of the individual to society, and (2) the standards for literacy that are established in society.

First, a critical literacy perspective challenges the assumption, sometimes implicit in the framing of literacy issues, that some individuals have "literacy-deficits" that need remediation. Under this assumption, literacy education is advocated as a response to a problem of inadequate "human capital" or "human resources." Literacy education in this context is seen as a means to transfer the literacy skills required for daily living and for employment to those with literacy deficits. While "skills transfer" is necessary, a critical literacy perspective suggests that some individuals lack literacy skills because of their systematic marginalization and discrimination in society. It is believed, therefore, that literacy education for such groups should provide reading and writing skills as a means for challenging society, and as a means for empowerment.

Second, a critical literacy perspective challenges assumptions about the standards for literacy that are established in society. Standards for expected levels of literacy are implicit in the reading and writing skills required for participation in a range of activities and societal institutions: reading a newspaper, participating in certain vocational training activities, reading and filling out applications for social assistance, reading documents of the court and other tribunals that constitute the justice system, etc. Specific standards for literacy are also implicit in the languages that are legitimated as the dominant means of communication in society. Literacy education in Canada often assumes that English or French are the most "functional" languages in which to read and write: thus they become de facto standards for literacy. This assumption, while valid, excludes the cultural realities of those outside of the dominant language groups, those who want to develop literacy skills in a different mother tongue, and those for whom sign language is their only or chosen form of communication. A critical literacy perspective, then, does not accept as given, or necessary, the standards of literacy that have come to prevail.

Methods for developing critical literacy begin with, and seek to validate, the stories, meanings, and experience of those who have been excluded from participation in society. Such methods are intended to change society by giving a "voice" and a place to those who have experienced exclusion. Through these methods the accepted standards for reading and writing are also challenged.

The difficulty with attempting to define literacy, and the source of controversy over the definition, is that once one takes seriously the relative nature of either the "functional" or the "critical" definitions, no universal definition of literacy is possible or desirable. The standard for a "literate" person varies de-

8

pending on the social and economic context, and the ends for which literacy is sought.

DEFINING LITERACY FOR ADULTS WITH A MENTAL HANDICAP

The definitions of literacy provided above are drawn from the "generic" literature on literacy. However, all of these definitions are useful in understanding the desire and possibilities for literacy among adults who have been labelled with a mental handicap. Adults, tutors, and program coordinators who were interviewed defined the kinds of literacy that have been sought, and the literacy programs to which a few adults with a mental handicap have had access.

For example, a few adults who have been labelled mentally handicapped are enrolled in adult basic education or upgrading classes offered at community colleges or provided through continuing education programs of school boards. The purpose of these programs is to provide them with basic and functional literacy skills. Other programs in the form of vocational and job-readiness training are meant in part to provide them with the literacy skills for acquiring and maintaining employment.[12] Some people participate in "learner-centred" community-based and volunteer tutoring programs designed to respond to what the individual learner identifies as his or her own literacy needs. These programs are guided by the goals of the individual and so assist him or her in developing a range of functional literacy skills for any number of activities. Through their participation in this kind of literacy education, adults with a mental handicap have developed a range of skills integral to increasing their independence in the community: reading bus schedules and labels on medication bottles; filling out forms for social assistance; reading books for pleasure; writing telephone messages; taking drivers' examinations; or simply signing their own name.[13] Some have gone on to write books describing their experiences and struggles in institutional care and the community. The stories that some individuals have written, and the books that have been published, are narratives about exclusion, rejection, sense of failure, abuse, and often hope. Such narratives fall clearly within the boundaries of what has been defined as critical literacy. The importance of such an approach to people with a disability is expressed in the following passage:

> When we listen to those who have been labelled "disabled" in this society, the concept of the importance of creating new language becomes more concrete. People who have been called "mentally retarded," for instance, want to create new language to describe their own experiences, and their demands to be treated as people first. They do not want reading material that fails to represent their experience accurately and further silences or stigmatizes them.[14]

In summary, the term "literacy" defies a singular definition. This is because individuals, governments, employers, social movements, and communities establish very diverse standards and purposes for the acquisition of literacy skills. There are two themes that underlie all three definitions of literacy. First, literacy, however it is defined, is a highly valued, some say essential skill that individuals require for participation in the social and economic life of the community. Second, literacy refers to a particular set of standards that must be met if individuals are to participate in various activities and institutions in society. Efforts to address the problem of literacy cannot only focus on transferring literacy skills to those who do not have them. As well, the standards our society sets for being able to read and write such official documents as court documents or social assistance forms need to be considered, challenged, and revised.

Notes

[1]Cited in The Provincial Literacy Advisory Committee, *Opening the Doors to Lifelong Learning: Empowering Undereducated Adults* (Victoria: British Columbia Ministry of Advanced Education, Training, and Technology, December 1989).

[2]James R. Patton and Edward A. Polloway, "Curricular Orientations," In Greg A. Robinson (ed.), *Best Practices in Mental Disabilities. Volume Two* (Eric Document Reproduction Service No. ED 304 830, 1988), p. 29.

[3]W.S. Gray, *The Teaching of Reading and Writing: An International Survey,* (Paris: UNESCO, 1956), p. 24.

[4]See for example Health and Welfare Canada. *Charting Canada's Future: A Report of the Demographic Review* (Ottawa: Minister of Supply and Services Canada, 1989).

[5]For a critique of this assumption see Kenneth Levine, "Functional Literacy: Fond Illusions and False Economies," *Harvard Educational Review,* Vol. 52, No. 3. (August 1982): 249-266.

[6]Newfoundland. *Education for Self-Reliance*, Education Report of the Royal Commission on Employment and Unemployment, (St. John's: 1985).

[7]Joseph Kozol, *Illiterate America* (New York: Doubleday, 1985).

[8]Woods Gordon Management Consultants, *The Cost of Illiteracy to Business in Canada,* for the Canadian Business Task Force on Literacy (Toronto: October 1987).

[9]C. Hunter and D. Harman, *Adult Illiteracy in the United States: A Report to the Ford Foundation* (New York: McGraw-Hill, 1979), p. 7.

[10]See Paulo Freire, *Pedagogy of the Oppressed,* Translated by Myra Bergman Ramos (New York: The Seabury Press, 1970).

[11]There are many texts which articulate the theory and practice of a critical literacy or pedagogy. For a few examples see Paulo Friere and Donaldo Macedo, *Literacy: Reading the Word and the World* (South Hadley, Mass.: Bergin and Harvey Publishers, 1987); Kathleen Rockhill, "Gender, Language and the Politics of Literacy," *British Journal of Sociology of Education,* 8(1987): 153-167; Magda Lewis and Roger Simon, "A Discourse Not Inteded for Her: Learning and Teaching within Patriarchy," *Harvard Educational Review,* 56(1986): 457-472; Michelle Sola and Adrian T. Bennett, "The Struggle for Voice: Literacy and Consciousness in an East Harlem School", *Journal of Education,* 167(1985): 88-110. Peter McLaren draws distinctions in the debate on literacy between functional literacy, cultural literacy, and critical literacy. He defines cultural literacy as the acquisition of the shared cultural values and knowledge which are considered necessary for participation in society. For the purposes of this overview, however, this approach to defining literacy can be encompassed within the definition of functional literacy. As McLaren acknowledges cultural literacy is one of the factors associated with functional literacy. See Peter McLaren, "Culture or Canon? Critical Pedagogy and the Politics of Literacy," *Harvard Educational Review,* Vol. 58 No. 2(May 1988): 213-234.

[12]One example of such a program is described in *Profile,* newsmagazine of the Metropolitan Toronto Association for Community Living, Spring 1990.

[13]Frontier College in Toronto, Ontario has been a pioneer both in developing a "learner-centred" approach to literacy, and in including adults with a mental handicap in literacy training. See Marsha Forest with Bruce Kappel, *It's About Learning: A Student Centred Approach to Adult Learning* (Toronto: Frontier College Press, 1988); Tracy Carpenter, *The Right to Read: Tutor's Handbook for SCIL Program: Student Centred Individualized Learning* (Toronto: Frontier College, 1986). See also The Scottish Community Education Council, *Moving Ahead: A new handbook for tutors helping mentally handicapped adults to learn* (Edinburgh, Scotland: 1987).

[14]In TVOntario, *Lifeline to Literacy: People With Disabilities Speak Out* (Toronto: The Ontario Education Communications Authority, 1989) p.13.

CHAPTER 2

MEASURING LITERACY AMONG ADULTS WITH A MENTAL HANDICAP

Three basic problems are encountered in measuring the level of literacy among adults with a mental handicap: (1) defining mental handicap; (2) sampling the adults in the population who have a mental handicap; and, (3) measuring levels of literacy.

DEFINING MENTAL HANDICAP

There is an inherent problem in studying any population including those adults who are identified as having a mental handicap. Establishing the parameters of the population often results in attributing generalized characteristics to what is in fact a very diverse group. While "mental handicap" is usually defined by impairments in intellectual capacity and adaptive behaviour that are evident at an early age, the concept is more a social construct than a fixed attribute or characteristic of individuals. As Rioux indicates, there is wide variation in the extent of impairments between individuals who are labelled mentally handicapped; the consequences of impairments vary in any individual depending on the learning processes in which they are engaged; and both the meaning and consequence of an impairment is contingent on the social demands placed on an individual.[1] Further, Szmanski has estimated that 75 to 90 percent of those labelled mentally handicapped have mild or borderline impairments.[2] Such findings and conclusions render the boundary between those who are labelled and those who are not, much less fixed than is often assumed.

SAMPLING

To measure the scale of the problem of illiteracy, a sample of the population(s) to be studied needs to be selected. Designing a sample of adults with a disability poses some difficulties. Two national surveys of adults with a disability, including adults with a mental handicap, have been carried out since 1983. For the 1986 Statistics Canada *Health and Activity Limitation Survey* (HALS), a sample was drawn from those who responded positively to the question on disability on the 1986 Census form. For those living in institutions and special care homes, etc., a sample was designed based on a list provided by the facility administration. One major difficulty with identifying a survey sample of adults with a disability is that individuals are required to "self-report" their disability. Because of the stigma associated with the labels of mental handicap or its synonym, "developmentally delayed" (the category used in the HALS survey), many individuals are reluctant to apply the term to themselves. A small field-test administered prior to the 1986 Census and HALS survey found that many persons with a "mild" disability would not answer positively to the question on disability.[3] Given estimates that those with a "mild" or "borderline" mental handicap make up 75 to 90 percent of this population, a significant sampling error can be expected. To offset this potential error, a small selection of those who responded "no" to the disability question was also included in the HALS sample. While it may be impossible to substantially reduce a sampling error of this nature, it is important to acknowledge the limitations of the data being used.

Another data base on people with a disability in Canada is the *Canadian Health and Disability Survey* (CHDS). This survey was attached as a supplement to the monthly Labour Force Survey sent to households in October 1983 and June 1984. The survey is subject to the same sampling limitations that arise from "self-reporting" a disability in other surveys.

There have been two national literacy surveys conducted in the past five years: the 1986 *Southam Literacy Survey*, and the 1989 Statistics Canada *Survey of Literacy Skills Used in Daily Activities*. In neither survey was the sample stratified to measure the level of literacy among people with a disability. The

Southam survey was administered to 2,398 adults aged eighteen and over who were randomly selected from 148 rural and urban communities across Canada. The sample for the Statistics Canada survey was not stratified according to disability because the respondents were selected from the monthly Labour Force Survey, which does not identify individuals according to disability.

While surveys on disability have inherent and probably intractable problems, this is not a reason for not carrying them out. Both the CHDS and HALS surveys have provided a data base to begin to systematically analyze issues of disability. However, such surveys provide only "crude" tools for measuring levels of literacy (highest level of schooling achieved), an issue to which the discussion now turns.

MEASURING LEVELS OF LITERACY

The difficulty in measuring the level of literacy in any particular population is finding a measure that can be sensitive to the different needs for literacy, while at the same time providing a standardized measure for the purposes of analysis. In the 1970s, attainment of grade 9 was selected by UNESCO as a measure of functional literacy, and many countries subsequently adopted this standard as their own.

The use of a standardized measure of literacy based on grade-level attainment poses substantial limitations to assessing the prevalence of levels of literacy in the population. As Blinn and Hody indicate:

> It is obvious that many people awarding themselves a Grade 5 or Grade 9 Certificate for the purpose of the census may not, in fact, have completed those grades, or, having once completed them, no longer know as much as when they did so. On the other hand, it is common knowledge that many persons with a low level of schooling are, in fact, very well educated: their level of schooling in no way reflects their knowledge or competence. We have no way of knowing how these figures balance out, or whether older people, who claim on the average a much lower level of schooling, in fact cannot read as

16

well as younger persons who attended schools where social promotion is the norm and where academic standards do not approach those of the era before the Second
World War.[4]

As well, Willinsky points to a number of studies that have
found that neither grade level and reading ability nor grade level
and reading activity necessarily correlate. In fact they are sometimes weakly correlated.[5]
  It is certain that any standardized measure of literacy will
be inherently insensitive to measuring functional levels of literacy: that is, a standardized measure will not capture the
variations in individual interests, cultures, occupations, geo-
graphical locations, and historical periods essential to the concept of functional literacy. It can be argued, nonetheless, that
some level of standardization in measurement is necessary to
carry out research and public policy development. Researchers
have focused more recently, therefore, on developing measures
more reflective of the functional definition of literacy than can be
provided by indicators of school attainment.
  The first large-scale Canadian survey of functional literacy skills that did not use grade level attainment as the measure,
was the Southam literacy study carried out in 1986.[6] The researchers sought an alternative to the grade 9 measure because
it was considered inadequate to assess the ability to function in
a "complex information society." The survey instrument was
adapted for the Canadian context from a U.S. survey.[7] Reading,
writing, and numeracy skills were tested by having respondents
answer questions about items found in everyday life such as road
signs, social insurance cards, and information on a bottle of
cough syrup. Ability to make calculations with regard to a lunch
menu or banking statement was also tested.
  The findings from the Southam survey estimated that 4.5
million or 24 percent of adult Canadians were functionally
illiterate. On a provincial basis, the illiteracy rate ranged from
a low of 17 percent in British Columbia to a high of 44 percent in
Newfoundland. The Southam survey found that 1.7 million of
those who were found to be "literate" would have been measured
as illiterate if the grade 9 school attainment measure had been

applied to them. Conversely, 2.4 million tested as "illiterate" on the Southam survey even though they had completed grade 9.[8] A literacy survey has more recently been carried out by Statistics Canada, entitled *Survey of Literacy Skills Used in Daily Activities*.[9] It was based on the assumption that while some standards are necessary for identifying the prevalence and nature of literacy, greater sensitivity to variation in levels of literacy can be achieved by avoiding measures that identify individuals as either functionally literate or functionally illiterate. For the purposes of the survey, literacy was defined as:

> the information processing skills necessary to use the **printed material** commonly encountered at work, at home and in the community.[10]

The design of the survey began with a conception of functional literacy skills as forming a continuum along which four levels of literacy could be identified. As in the Southam survey, test items were selected to demonstrate functional literacy skills. The survey was administered to a much larger sample than the Southam survey (approx. 9,500 and 2,398 individuals respectively). Individuals who attained either level 1 or 2 on the continuum of four levels of literacy were considered to possess inadequate literacy skills to "deal with the majority of written material encountered in everyday life." This group constitutes 16 percent of the total adult population (those between ages sixteen and sixty-nine). This figure is substantially lower than the 24 percent "functionally illiterate" rate found among adults (eighteen years old and over) in the Southam survey. However, the 16 percent figure does not incorporate analysis of the survey of writing and numeracy skills which had not been released when this study was carried out.

These surveys indicate that there is increasing sophistication in methods for determining functional literacy. As well, procedures for designing a representative sample have allowed for more precise measurement of levels of literacy for certain "populations." These include the general adult population, and major stratifications within it (by gender, ethnicity, socio-economic status, educational background, and region). However, these

18

samples have not been designed to measure levels of literacy among adults with a disability.

LEVELS OF LITERACY AMONG ADULTS WITH A MENTAL HANDICAP

It is not possible with existing data sources to measure the prevalence of literacy among adults with a mental handicap as accurately as is possible with other populations. The only measures of prevalence that are available for this group are the conventional measures of school attainment. Besides the inherent limitations of this standard when applied to the general population, there are even greater difficulties in its use when assessing adults with a mental handicap. First, because of their label, or their disabling condition, or both, most adults with a mental handicap have not progressed through the regular school system. Second, for those who have, there is no data confirming the extent to which attainment of grade 9 is a valid indicator of functional reading or writing skills. Third, many have gone to special schools. Some enrollment data is available for this group. However, there may be little equivalence in grade level with the regular school system. Fourth, others have lived in institutional facilities for long periods of time with little or no attachment to the educational system.

The following table presents percentages of adults with a mental handicap who can be identified as lacking "functional literacy" using the grade 9 attainment measure and data from the Health and Activity Limitation Survey.

Table 1
Education Level of Adults With a Mental Handicap
Aged 15 and Over

Highest education level	% of adults with a mental handicap
No schooling	25
Grade 5 to Grade 8	41
Grade 9 to Grade 13	27
Some Post-Secondary	7

SOURCE: Health and Activity Limitation Survey, 1986.

The data indicates that 66 percent of adults with a mental handicap have achieved less than a grade 9 level of education. Therefore, they have a rate of literacy that is significantly below that of the general adult population in Canada. While this data suggests there is an extremely high rate of illiteracy among adults with a mental handicap, this cannot, for reasons cited above, be considered to be a completely valid estimate of functional literacy for this group. If the test-items used in the recent Statistics Canada survey of literacy skills had been systematically applied to a sample of adults with a mental handicap, distribution of the levels of literacy among this group may have provided an entirely different picture. We simply do not know.

The statistical data sources available on the characteristics of adults with a disability, and on levels of literacy, are not compatible. This reflects the similar lack of connection evident in the wider literature in these two areas. Until samples of the population who have a disability are included in surveys on literacy, the ability to analyze how issues of literacy affect this group will be much more limited than it need be. Consequently, neither the problem nor the solutions will be fully appreciated.

Notes

[1]Cited in Charlene Senn, *Vulnerable: Sexual abuse and people with an intellectual impairment* (Toronto: The G. Allan Roeher Institute 1988), p. vii.

[2]*Ibid.*, p. 6.

[3]Statistics Canada, *The Health and Activity Limitation Survey User's Guide* (Ottawa: June 1988), p. 2.

[4]Cited in John C. Cairns, *Adult Illiteracy in Canada* (Toronto: Council of Ministers of Education, February 1988), p. 5.

[5]John Willinsky, "The Construction of a Crisis: Literacy in Canada," *Canadian Journal of Education*, 15, 1(1990): 1-15.

[6]Creative Research Group, *Literacy in Canada: A research report* (Ottawa: Southam News, 1987).

[7]The U.S. survey was carried out for the National Assessment of Educational Progress (NEAP).

[8]While the survey challenged the school attainment standard of literacy it imposed another. A twenty-five person "jury" meant to be representative of both expert opinion and the general population was used to select the items for which individuals would have to get correct answers in order to be identified as "literate". There was significant variation in selections by the jury. In order to come up with a measure for analyzing the survey, the researchers used the items on which there was most consensus by the jury. It was then determined by the researchers that a minimum of 80 percent correct answers on these items was required for individuals to measure as literate. Having analyzed the methodology for the design and analysis of the survey Willinsky observed:

> The jury method has been used in other studies of language issues, although it often illustrates the thin

veneer of linguistic consensus that sustains the concept
of a standard in the language... It should remind us that
we do not, nor seem to need to, share a precise standard
for a concept such as "literacy".

See John Willinsky, "The Construction of a Crisis: Literacy in
Canada," p. 4.

[9]Statistics Canada, *Survey of Literacy Skills Used in Daily Activities: Survey Overview* (Ottawa: 1990).

[10]*Ibid.*, p. 1.

CHAPTER 3

THE NEED FOR LITERACY

In recent years goals have been articulated for including individuals with a mental handicap in all dimensions of community life. A commitment to these goals has been expressed by advocacy groups, service agencies, local, provincial, and national Associations for Community Living, and governments. Accordingly, policy and program analysis has increasingly turned toward the systemic barriers to inclusion in the community, and toward the denials of social justice and human rights to individuals with a mental handicap. The need for literacy has not figured largely in this analysis, however. This chapter looks at four ways in which literacy is central to achieving current, widely-held goals:

- enabling participation in the community
- addressing poverty
- accessing employment
- securing social justice and human rights

PARTICIPATION IN COMMUNITY LIFE

The need for literacy among adults with a mental handicap is likely to become intensely evident as adults move from institutional care to the community, and as their integration in the community is more aggressively sought. This is because, more and more, literacy is a requirement of managing daily life and effectively participating in the community. Print information is now pervasive in society. In a "community" in which this is the case, literacy becomes the means for carrying out what Levine has identified as the "transactions of information and knowledge" which "an individual wishes - or is compelled - to engage."[1] Yet despite the requirements for literacy, and despite the very low levels of literacy among adults with a mental handicap, their need for literacy has not been widely articulated by those who advocate on their behalf. Nor has it been articulated by those who advocate on behalf of those labelled as "illiterate", or by those who carry out research and analysis in the field of mental handicap.

Why is it that issues of literacy and mental handicap have not received the attention they may well deserve? One reason may be that other issues faced by adults with a mental handicap, and the needs they have for support, can seem so overwhelming that literacy becomes of secondary importance, or is not considered to be a need at all. While it is understandable that such a view may prevail, it is important to point out its weaknesses. First, literacy cannot be separated from the social and life skills which are seen to be essential if adults with a mental handicap are to participate and be more fully included in the community. Second, literacy cannot be separated from the issues of poverty, unemployment, social justice, and human rights —issues at the forefront of the agenda for change. (These issues are examined in later sections in this chapter.)

Social skills can be defined as those needed to manage relationships with people. Life skills can be defined as those needed to manage the activities of independent daily life. While there is a recognition of the need for many adults with a mental handicap to develop these skills, there is very little literature which explicity relates their development to literacy skills. The Scottish Community Education Council has provided one framework to identify the range of literacy skills that are required by adults with a mental handicap to develop their social skills and life skills, and thereby to increase their participation in the community.[2] The framework provides an analysis which has three basic steps:

1. Identify the settings or relationships in which an individual is or will be involved (whether leisure,

job, private life, or coping with shopping, housing, finances, etc.).
2. Identify the situations that will be encountered in each setting and the activities that will be carried out ("home" for instance can include such activities as reading for leisure, cleaning, cooking, budgeting, planning leisure, etc.)
3. Specify the reading, writing, and numeracy skills that will be required for each activity ("cooking" for instance can require reading labels for ingredients and recipes, and using numbers in measuring amounts and setting temperatures).

The more that adults become integrated in the community, and the more that opportunities are provided for them to make decisions and to gain independence, the more likely it is that they will encounter print information. Many adults, including those with a mental handicap, have not had the opportunity to develop the level of literacy skill required to deal with this information. Analysis of the readability of product warning labels, for example, indicates that most key words on labels require between grade 4 and grade 10.[3] Such findings imply that literacy skills need to be enhanced. These findings also suggest that the standards of literacy for consuming medical and health-related information need to be challenged. The same would likely hold true of many other kinds of information encountered in daily activities.

There is considerable potential for literacy to become a means for achieving the goals of community integration and increasing independence for adults with a mental handicap. One of the few reviews on literacy issues and adults with a mental handicap suggests that literacy is not only a means to increased "competence" in the community. It is also a means of access to experiences of daily life which many adults have been denied because of the protective nature of the environments in which they have lived.[4]

26

POVERTY

Many studies point to a relationship between low levels of literacy and poverty. For example, the national survey on literacy by Southam News found that the personal income reported by those identified as literate was 44 percent higher than the personal income reported by those identified as illiterate. The income gap between the literate and illiterate over age fifty-five was almost 100 percent. For those between eighteen and thirty-four the gap was 13 percent.

A more recent survey by Statistics Canada found that those with the highest level of literacy are more likely to have high incomes than low incomes. The study found that 54 percent of those earning less than $10,000 achieved high scores on literacy tests. Comparatively, 82 percent of those with an annual income of $40,000 or over achieved a similar score.

Adults with a mental handicap are most likely to be poor. Analysis of the data from the *Health and Activity Limitation Survey* found that 89 percent of adults with a mental handicap had an annual income of less than $10,000. Illiteracy contributes to poverty in large part because an individual who has very few literacy skills is much less likely to obtain employment that pays wages above the poverty line. However, for adults with a mental handicap increased levels of literacy may or may not improve employment opportunities. The impact depends on the extent to which literacy skills can be acquired by any particular individual, on the kinds of skills that the labour market demands, and on the ability and willingness of employers to make the work setting accessible to people with a disability.

Even if increased literacy skills can widen employment opportunities for a person with a disability, paid employment will not necessarily eradicate his or her poverty. The high percentage of people with a disability who have low incomes suggests that those who are in the labour force are paid at or near the minimum wage. Despite receiving some benefits for disability-related costs, 40 percent of adults with a disability report out-of-pocket expenses related to their disabling condition.[5] For those unable to participate in the paid labour force for whatever reason, inadequate income assistance and disability-related benefits are found to be significant factors in their chronic poverty.[6]

While illiteracy is one factor affecting poverty, it is also a factor which exacerbates the consequences of poverty. One of the most important consequences of poverty is the greater likelihood of lower health status.[7] For those who are poor and who lack literacy skills, their health status is in "double jeopardy": not only are they more likely to suffer the consequences of poor living conditions, but because of low levels of literacy they may not be able to access information to assist them in changing some of the conditions in which they live. A recent survey by Frontier College and the Ontario Public Health Association, for example, showed that people with lower levels of reading skills tend to rate their health status as only fair or poor four times as often as people with a university education. The study suggests that literacy is a health issue because of the importance of reading skills for such tasks as reading medication labels, getting information about work safety, nutrition, and child care.[8]

EMPLOYMENT

Literacy has been found to be one factor which significantly affects access to paid employment. A 1985 study on educationally disadvantaged adults in Canada reported, for instance, that those with less than a grade 9 education (the measure of functional illiteracy commonly used) constituted more than 20 percent of the population in Maritime provinces. Sixty percent of this group were not in the labour force.[9] Does this relationship between literacy and employment status hold true for adults with a mental handicap? We do know that people with a disability are much less likely to be attached to the paid labour force than people without a disability. As Table 2 indicates it is estimated that only 25 percent of adults with a mental handicap have paid employment.

28

TABLE 2
Labour Force Status Of Adults with a Mental Handicap
Aged 15 And Over

Labour force status	Sex		Total
	Female (%)	Male (%)	%
Seniors	8	6	7
Employed	22	27	25
Unemployed	3	5	4
Not in the labour force*	62	56	59
Unknown	5	6	5
Total	100	100	100

SOURCE: Health and Activity Limitation Survey, 1986.
have not been employed for at least a year or more.

In considering how literacy affects access to paid employment for people with a disability, it is important first to establish,
in general terms, how literacy affects access to paid employment.
There are two ways: (1) through the educational qualifications
that are obtained in the process of gaining literacy skills; and (2)
through the level of literacy skills which are required for per-
forming job tasks. Access to the paid labour force requires
increasingly higher levels of educational qualification and certi-
fication. A study that reviewed editions of the Dictionary of
Occupational Titles published by the Department of Labour in
the United States is instructive in this regard. The study found
fewer changes in the job descriptions of occupations in successive
editions of the Dictionary, than changes in the required qualifications.[10] The Canadian Business Task Force on Literacy also
reports that a minimum of grade 12 is now required by many
corporations just for entry level jobs.[11] The kinds and level of
literacy skills an individual possesses also affects access to paid

employment. A study by Mikulecky, for example, suggests that 85 percent of jobs now require some reading skills at a grade 9 level or higher.[12]

Given the impact of one's level of literacy on access to the labour market, and the low rate of labour force participation of adults with a disability, increasing the levels of literacy among this group appears to be of critical importance. As Table 3 suggests, there is some evidence that the education level achieved affects on labour force status of adults with a mental handicap: the higher the level of education achieved, the more likely it is that adults will be employed.

TABLE 3

Education Level and Labour Force Status Of Adults With a Mental Handicap (Age 15 and Over)

EDUCATION LEVEL	% ADULTS EMPLOYED	%NOT EMPLOYED*	UNKNOWN
No school to grade 8	21	73	6
Grade 9 to 13	31	65	4
Some post-secondary	37	60	3

SOURCE: Health and Activity Limitation Survey, 1986.
*Unemployed, not in the labour force, or seniors.

However, more than the level of literacy will need to change if access to employment opportunities for this group is to be increased. The statistical data on education levels, disability, and employment suggest that there is a much weaker relationship between education levels and employment for adults with a disability, than for adults in the general population. Thirty-one percent of adults with a disability who have a secondary education level are in the paid labour force. Sixty-one percent of adults with the same level of education, but who do not have a disability, are in the paid labour force.[13] While many people with a disability are employable, and have high levels of education, low levels of

30

participation in the paid labour force persist for this group. This fact has been attributed to such factors as lack of on-the-job supports, lack of transportation, and physical and social barriers at the employment setting.

Although there may be structural barriers to employment for adults with a disability, beyond a lack of literacy skills, other factors that may widen employment opportunities need to be taken into account:

- an anticipated labour shortage (the impact of which cannot be definitively assessed in terms of adults with a mental handicap);

- a growing service sector that does not necessarily require high levels of literacy;

- employment equity legislation and requirements;

- human rights legislation prohibiting discrimination based on mental handicap and requiring employers to make reasonable accommodations for employees;

- opportunities to develop skills in computer literacy; and,

- commitments by employers to making their workplaces more accessible.

Some educators interviewed for this study indicated that certain individuals with a mental handicap can improve their literacy skills to such an extent that it will make a difference in the job skills they have at their disposal, and therefore will make a difference in their employability. However, they also indicated that, in their experience, some adults are not able to develop sufficient literacy skills to make an appreciable difference in the kinds of jobs in which they can be employed. It was suggested, nonetheless, that even small improvements in literacy skills can enable or increase the participation of adults in employment. For instance, literacy can provide an individual with the basic skills to manage the transportation system in order to get to work, to read instructions at the work setting, to participate in social activities in the work setting, and to manage personal finances.

In summary, low levels of literacy can have a significant impact on poverty, unemployment, and lower health status for the general population. People with a disability are much more vulnerable to the incidence of all these factors in their lives than people without a disability. However, for increased levels of literacy to have an impact on the quality of life of people with a disability, other barriers to employment and adequate income must also be addressed.

SOCIAL JUSTICE AND HUMAN RIGHTS

In recent years literacy has emerged as an issue of social justice and of human rights. This is in part because poverty, unemployment, and lower health status are increasingly seen to be personal costs that come with low levels of literacy. Literacy is seen as a social justice issue because literacy skills, access to literacy education, and the personal costs of illiteracy are distributed unevenly, some would say unfairly, in the population. Literacy has become an issue of human rights because the lack of literacy can limit the enjoyment of individual's equality, legal, and citizenship rights.

Social or distributive justice is concerned with how to achieve fairness in the distribution of society's resources and benefits. One principle of distributive justice requires that resources should be allocated in ways that benefit the least advantaged in society.[14] Drawing on this principle, Stevens has argued that allocation of resources to adult basic education can be justified for those adults who were excluded from schooling or whose level of literacy was so low that:

> it [is] an obstacle to the exercise of the rights of citizenship, the opportunity for economic advancement, and the attainment of self-respect. Thus social/educational programs designed to remediate adult literacy [could] be justified, not simply from the viewpoint of utility, but from the standpoint of social justice.[15]

32

Stevens has also argued that literacy is not a fundamental human right belonging to the "human condition," but is a right that enables the "operation of more basic human and constitutional rights." In a similar vein Oxenham suggests that if:

> we regard literacy as a right contingent upon the cir-
> cumstances of a given society, we would be obliged to
> identify rights which every individual should enjoy, but
> would not be able to - either wholly or in part - unless he
> were sufficiently literate... A society where a ... 'demo-
> cratic' view prevails would doubtless aver that ... every-
> body should be enabled to become literate.[16]

The kinds of rights that require some level of literacy if they are to be fully enjoyed are many. The right of citizens to participate in government elections, to enter into contractual agreements, to challenge the violation of their human rights through human rights commissions may be most fully enjoyed only if they have achieved certain standards of literacy. The extent to which individuals enjoy these rights may also depend on the extent to which they have developed literacy skills.

That individuals should have a "right to literacy" is a principle now commonly found in statements on literacy, education generally, and adult education in particular. One of the first "declarations" of right to literacy was made at the 1975 International Symposium for Literacy in Persepolis, Iran. Known as the "Persepolis Declaration", it stated:

> Literacy is not an end in itself. It is a fundamental
> human right.[17]

A dozen years later, the declaration and recommendations from the International Literacy Seminar in Toronto stated:

> Literacy is a basic human right for the advancement of
> all people around the world...
>
> Justice demands that the problem of illiteracy must be

Literacy and Labels

attacked in a world that possesses all the means and resources to do so...

In order to promote social justice and equality, the special needs of oppressed people must be recognized and
met in literacy programs. This includes: women, in-
digenous peoples, minorities, the unemployed, and
people who have been labelled and excluded.[18]

There are three ways in which issues of literacy, disability,
social justice, and human rights can be formulated.
First, the distribution of literacy skills in the population is
linked to how resources are allocated to education of both children and adults. A "fair" distribution of educational resources
and literacy skills is thus related to the "particular concepts of
distrbutive justice that guides political and economic policies."[19]
That people with a disability are often systematically excluded
from opportunities to gain literacy skills is one aspect of their
unfair and unequal treatment.[20]   Second, individuals with a
mental handicap have historically been excluded from enjoyment of citizenship, legal, and equality rights.[21] While there are
now protections of such rights, literacy skills may be an important factor in ensuring that individuals are able to enjoy their
rights. Literacy can also assure the ability to challenge discrimination through human rights commissions, administrative tribunals, and the courts.
Third, in order for individuals with a disability to exercise
their rights they may need to use appeal boards, courts, human
rights commissions, etc. The standards for literacy established
for using these systems (standards for reading and understanding court documents, procedural information, filling in forms,
etc.) need to be examined and possibly changed. Current standards pose barriers to the effective use of these systems by some
adults with a mental handicap.[22]

The research and analysis presented in this chapter suggests that literacy is a key factor in achieving greater inclusion
of adults with a mental handicap in the community.
First, literacy has been identified as a factor that enables

participation in community life. Many of the skills required by adults with a mental handicap to further their participation and independence in the community are skills that, at their roots, are related in some way to literacy. It could be argued, therefore, that access to literacy is important in achieving the goals of integration in community life for adults with a mental handicap.

Second, research has identified the close relationship between low levels of literacy, poverty, unemployment, and low health status. These factors are found to prevail among the population with a disability to a significantly greater degree than among the general population. Increasing the levels of literacy among this group is likely to have a significant impact on their quality of life. At the same time, factors that consign individuals with a disability to a life of unemployment, poverty, and low health status will not be ameliorated simply by higher levels of literacy. Other barriers encountered by individuals with a disability must also be accounted for: barriers to adequate income and income assistance, to the educational system and educational qualifications, and to the labour market.

Third, many have argued that literacy is required to achieve justice for individuals. It is argued that because literacy is a "good" in society, because it enables the enjoyment of other benefits, and because it is required to some extent for the enjoyment of equality, citizenship and legal rights, then the greatest degree of equity in access to literacy skills should be promoted. Standards established for literacy may also pose unnecessary barriers to the justice system and to the exercise of individual rights. With a social justice and human rights perspective it could be argued that the extent to which adults with a mental handicap are systematically excluded from access to literacy is precisely the extent to which they are treated inequitably in and by society.

Notes

[1]See Kenneth Levine, *The Social Context of Literacy* (London: Routledge & Kegan Paul, 1986).

[2]See The Scottish Community Education Council, *Moving Ahead: A new handbook for tutors helping mentally handicapped adults to learn.*

[3]Donna Fletcher and Doris Abood, "An Analysis of the Readability of Product Warning Labels: Implications for Curriculum Development for Persons with Moderate and Severe Mental Retardation," *Education and Training in Mental Retardation* (September, 1988): p. 224-227.

[4]Adult Literacy and Basic Skills Unit, *Literacy and Numeracy Work with Mentally Handicapped Adults* (London: February 1982), p. 10.

[5]Magda K. Hamilton, "The Health and Activity Limitation Survey," in Statistics Canada, *Health Reports*, Vol 1. No. 2 (1989) p. 184.

[6]See Sherri Torjman *Income Insecurity: The Disability Income System in Canada* (Toronto: The G. Allan Roeher Institute, 1988). p. 9-37.

[7]National Health and Welfare Canada. *Achieving Health for All* (Ottawa: Minister of Supply and Services Canada, 1986).

[8]Frontier College and the Ontario Public Health Association, *Literacy and Health: Phase I, Making the World Healthier and Safer for People who can't Read* (Toronto: Ontario Public Health Association, 1989).

[9]Cited in John Cairns, *Adult Illiteracy in Canada*, p. 17.

[10]David Harman, *Illiteracy: A National Dilemma* (New York: Cambridge Book Company, 1987), p. 54.

[11]See Woods Gordon Management Consultants, *The Cost of Illiteracy to Business in Canada,* for the Canadian Business Task Force on Literacy.

36

[12]Cited in Woods Gordon Management Consultants, *The Cost of Illiteracy to Business in Canada,* p. 13.

[13]This data is presented in D. Gower, *Labour market activity of disabled persons in Canada* (Ottawa: Statistics Canada, April 1988). These results are from the Canadian Health and Disability Survey.

[14]This principle of justice has been extensively elaborated in John Rawls, *A Theory of Justice* (Cambridge, Mass.: Harvard University Press, 1971).

[15]Edward W. Stevens, Jr., *Literacy, Law, and Social Order,* (DeKalb, Illinois: Northern Illinois University Press, 1988), p. 41.

[16]Stevens draws on Oxenham in his argument. This quote was taken from John Oxenham, *Literacy: Writing, reading and social organisation* (London: Routledge and Kegan Paul, 1980), p. 85.

[17]The full text of the Persepolis Declaration can be found in Leon Bataille, ed., *A Turning Point for Literacy*, Proceedings of the International Symposium for Literacy, Persepolis, Iran, 3-8 September, 1975 (New York: Pergamon Press), p. 273-277.

[18]This position is stated in the report of the workshop proceedings in *Literacy in Industrialized Countries: A Focus on Practice,* Margaret Gayfer (ed.), (Toronto: 1988), p. 11-12.

[19]Stevens, *Literacy, Law, and Social Order,* p. 22.

[20]Margaret Gayfer (ed.), *Literacy in Industrialized Countries: A Focus on Practice.*

[21]See Marcia Rioux, *Last in the Queue,* A speech presented to The International Association for the Scientific Study of Mental Deficiency, Dublin, Ireland, August 1988 (Toronto: The G. Allan Roeher Institute, 1989).

[22]See Denis Morrice, "In the courtroom, disability means more than ramps and wheelchairs," *The Globe and Mail* 27 July 1989.

CHAPTER 4

LEARNING, LITERACY, AND MENTAL HANDICAP

Like any other adults, adults with a mental handicap benefit from having literacy skills. The preceding chapter outlined various dimensions of their need for literacy. The prevalence of illiteracy among adults with a mental handicap, however, is significantly higher than the prevalence among the general population. How is this fact to be explained? It is commonly assumed that there are lower levels of literacy among adults with a mental handicap precisely because they have a mental handicap. This assumption leads to the conclusion that an adult with a mental handicap is the "problem": he or she possesses inherent and fixed intellectual "deficits" that prevent the development of adequate literacy skills. The analysis provided in this chapter suggests that this assumption, and the conclusion that follows from it, is erroneous.

Three main findings from the research are presented in this chapter:

• adults with a mental handicap can learn literacy skills;

• the failure to develop literacy skills is explained to a significant degree by their lack of opportunity to develop effective learning strategies;

• development of effective learning strategies depends on the degree to which adults are supported to exercise autonomy in various aspects of their lives, and on the instructional approach in the learning process.

THE CAPACITY TO LEARN

Many who were interviewed felt that when the right conditions were in place, adults with a mental handicap could develop literacy skills. All agreed that adults with a mental handicap generally take a longer time to learn to read and write. The pace of learning is often slower than with other adults, and consequently, sometimes very frustrating for both the adult learner and the educator. Because the vast majority of individuals with a mental handicap have what has been identified as "mild" or "moderate" impairment, it is only a very small minority who may not be able to develop literacy skills at all. Some of those who have been labelled as "severely" or "profoundly" handicapped have, nonetheless, learned to read and write.

Extensive research in the field of mental handicap has demonstrated that the existence in an individual of the condition labelled as "mental handicap" does not mean he or she is unable to learn in general, or to learn literacy skills in particular. Whitman and other researchers are redefining the meaning of mental handicap, shifting away from conceptions that focus on fixed and unchanging "intellectual deficits." Whitman suggests that one conclusion to be drawn from research in the field is that the "critical defining characteristic of persons with mental retardation [sic] is not their adaptive behaviour or cognitive deficiencies, which can be remediated".[1] The critical variable in learning is not the presence or absence of the condition of mental handicap. Rather, the critical variable is whether or not an individual uses effective learning strategies (also termed as cognitive strategies). Adults with a mental handicap tend to use ineffective strategies. As a result accomplishing learning tasks (like reading or writing) or achieving learning goals is more difficult. And while adults with a mental handicap may be able to learn new skills in a training situation, it has been found that without effective learning strategies they tend to have difficulty transferring these skills to a non-training setting where instructional supports or cues have been removed.[2] Researchers have also pointed to memory "deficits" as characteristic of individuals with a mental handicap.[3] "Memory" refers to capacities to acquire, retain, and retrieve information and knowledge. Without effective learning strategies, adults also have difficulty with tasks associated with memory.[4] The capacity for using memory is integral to skills like reading and writing.

Research in the field of mental handicap, reading disability, and literacy in general, is increasingly turning toward the nature of learning strategies, and the means by which effective strategies can be developed.[5] The results of such research indicate that in many instances individuals, including those with a mental handicap, can develop effective learning strategies that help them to achieve their learning goals.[6]

LEARNING STRATEGIES

A "learning strategy" or a "cognitive strategy" has been defined as "an activity undertaken by a person for the purpose of coping with the requirements of a task";[7] as a "a planned design for controlling and manipulating certain information";[8] and, as "a pattern of decisions in the acquisition, retention, and utilization of information".[9] With respect to literacy, learning strategies are required to manage the "tasks" of reading, writing, and using numbers. These tasks involve dealing with print and numerical "information." They also involve drawing on and applying the "information" an individual has about his or her own skills, previous experiences, history, and interests.

Many kinds of learning strategies are used in reading, writing, and numeracy. Transferring, for example, is the strategy of carrying over previously learned knowledge to a new learning event. Comprehension in reading requires the use of prior knowledge and experiences to obtain meaning from reading texts, and to bring meaning to one's writing: prior knowledge has to be "transferred" into a new reading or writing situation. Generalization or metacognitive strategies are strategies in which higher order categories are used to organize specific information or lower-order categories (for instance, being able to classify "dog" under the category "animal"). These strategies are essential for processing the information encountered and used in reading, writing, and numeracy. Strategies for "discrimination" between objects and shapes, for "remembering," for "prediction" of patterns or plots in reading, and for "sequencing" or ordering information are also essential to becoming literate.[10]

Given a general recognition that learning strategies are integral to literacy, research is now turning to identifying the factors that explain why adults with a mental handicap, even though they have the capacity, have tended not to use or to develop effective strategies. The research identifies two factors that affect the development of learning strategies among adults with a mental handicap: (1) the fostering of dependent relationships; and (2) the instructional approach.

The fostering of dependency

Researchers in the field suggest that one of the most important factors in explaining why adults tend not to use or develop effective learning strategies is that they have been encouraged to become or remain "dependent." Shapiro, for example, suggests that individuals with a mental handicap become passive and dependent learners in large part because of society's low expectations of their abilities.[11] Whitman argues that dependence is not "inextricably linked to retardation, but rather is a function of a variety of potentially remediable factors such as inappropriate demands by others, overprotective parents, and the absence of experiences that foster decision-making."[12] In this view, dependence results from the control that others have over an individual's life. As Martin and Mithaug indicate, individuals become passive learners when they are instructed "on what to do when and how to do it."[13] In relation to literacy, one literacy educator who was interviewed summarized in the following way:

> To acquire literacy skills, individuals must be able to define their goals for becoming literate. Yet many adults with a mental handicap have never really had the power to define their own goals. They have become used to being told what they should learn.

To develop and use effective learning strategies, researchers have argued that individuals with a mental handicap must be given the opportunity, the encouragement, and the skills to be "self-controlling," "self-managing," and "self-regulating." A conclusion to be drawn from this research is that the capacity to develop literacy, and the learning strategies associated with it, is related to the opportunity to exercise autonomy. As long as adults lack the opportunity to exercise autonomy in their lives, the development of their literacy skills will continue to be hindered.

Such a conclusion is sobering. While many adults with a mental handicap may be able to develop literacy skills, they are caught in what might be called a "cycle of dependency." Many are placed in relationships that foster their dependence on others, whether at home, in training settings, or in leisure settings. Poverty, unemployment, and lower health status all contribute to this dependency. The degree to which literacy education can, by itself, break this cycle of dependency, and assist adults to develop effective learning strategies, remains a compelling but unanswered question.

The instructional approach

Instructional approaches, whether in literacy education or other educational or training settings, have an impact on the capacity of adults with a mental handicap to develop learning strategies, and to learn to carry out certain tasks. Instructional approaches, themselves, can foster dependence and hinder learning. Some researchers in the field of mental handicap have pointed out that where instructors control the learning situation few opportunities are provided to foster "self-control" —a pre-requisite for effective learning strategies.[14] For instance, one study showed that the "threat of evaluation," which can be seen as a measure of external control by instructors, had a negative impact on the oral reading performance of individuals with a mental handicap.[15]

Forest identifies one of the key elements in learning to read and write as the ability of educators to assist adult learners in developing learning strategies. She writes: "Teachers must stop putting barriers in the way of reading. They must stop fracturing language into abstract letters, sounds, words and help readers build strategies to find meaning which is relevant, interesting and real in written language."[16] Other research suggests that instructional approaches must "cede control from the external socialization agent (expert) to the person [with a mental handicap]."[17] This is seen as a necessary step to enable individuals with a mental handicap to develop effective learning strategies and to overcome the kinds of limitations to learning that they commonly experience: difficulty in maintaining learning, in generalizing learning to non-training settings, and in retaining and recalling information and knowledge. These limitations can pose significant barriers to developing and using literacy skills because adult learners continually encounter new situations of reading and writing outside of the relationship with an instructor or tutor. Every new book, sign, label, form, and personal letter presents a new situation to the reader and writer. Based on her experience in teaching literacy to adults with a mental handicap, Doré also suggests that a critical step in solving problems of low self-esteem, passivity and the lack of self-direction on the part of some adult learners, is the enabling and sustaining of their personal autonomy.[18] In order to enable personal autonomy, her pedagogical or instructional approach lies with what has been defined in this study as "critical literacy." It focuses on "conscientization", a process of learning to be conscious about what one lives, feels, is, and what one wishes to do. While such an approach can bear significant advances, she also points to the real challenges that educators face: slow progress, the need to individualize and adapt curriculum, as well as behavioural challenges that some adults present.[19]

DEVELOPING EFFECTIVE LEARNING STRATEGIES

The research suggests there are four steps to developing effective learning strategies. These concern:

- **identification of learning goals** which the learner wishes to pursue

- **analysis of tasks** to be carried out in achieving reading and writing goals

- **selection of methods** for learning the tasks of reading, writing, and numeracy

- **monitoring and assessment** of the learning process and literacy skills developed

Identification of goals and tasks

The first step in developing effective learning strategies is for the learner to specify why literacy is important to him or her. Literature and research in both the field of mental handicap and in literacy education have stressed that it is critical for the learner to be involved in defining the goals and the tasks for which literacy is sought. This has been advocated for a number of reasons.

First, the need for literacy varies according to the individuals, their interests, and the context in which they will use their literacy skills (for example, goals could include to become more employable; to read a bus schedule, labels on food packages in a grocery store, a novel; to write a letter). Literacy becomes relevant to a particular individual when it is related to his or her own needs and goals. Given that many adults with a mental handicap have been rendered dependent on others to make decisions for them, the challenge for literary educators is to encourage them to articulate, for themselves, their wishes and needs.

Second, researchers have found that the significance and relevance of the task to the individual (whether it is related to literacy or otherwise) is a critical variable in determining the extent to which an individual will learn. Campione, for instance, has postulated that individuals with a mental handicap may not produce effective learning strategies when they do not understand the "significance" of a task, thereby inhibiting their learning capacity.[20] Bray and Turner make a similar point, and suggest that "a strategy is always adopted in response to the subject's [the individual's] understanding of the problem."[21] It can be concluded that the capacity of adults to learn is related to the extent to which they have an opportunity to choose to learn what is important to them.

Third, literacy educators indicate that reading, writing,

and numeracy skills only develop in the context of the intentions and meanings that the learner brings to bear on a text. Carpenter identifies the "key" to learning how to read and write as "building meaning." She writes: "Learning must remain in the hands and minds of learners. They have a lifetime of thoughts that can come pouring forth if trust is developed."[22] And Lytle writes: "We now understand more about the significant role of a reader's or writer's prior knowledge in acquiring and developing literacy, and we recognize that ... meanings are made in the context of prior meanings."[23] Adult learners who were interviewed for this study also indicated that it was difficult to engage in learning when the reading or writing task was un-related to their own experience or interests. One woman who was interviewed said:

> The first [reading] program I went to [the teacher] started me with kindergarten. They started on apple - "say apple". My god, I thought I'm back in school. Their treating me like I'm "retarded" again... [At the volunteer tutor program] they treat you like an adult. They ask you what you would like to read. They sit with you. There was no rights or wrongs. I used to feel really stupid. But they [tutors] said they were going to learn from us. They learn what its like at the other end of the table. Now I know that I can do anything I want.

And a man who had had some literacy education said:

> Some books they use for teaching reading seem awfully childish. I don't want to read this - it's a bunch of junk. Whereas if you're interested in it... For myself I was interested in architectural drafting. I learned faster because that was what I wanted to learn how to do. We're forgetting to ask people. We're making too many assumptions. People should be tied into what they want to do.

Analysis of tasks
In Chapter Three, a framework was outlined for identifying the

social and life skills that individuals may want to develop, the literacy requirements that underlie the use of such skills, and the particular reading and writing skills associated with these requirements. This "mapping" approach assists learners and literacy educators in identifying the particular steps that can be followed in gaining literacy. In this framework, the analysis proceeds from general learning goals to specific task requirements. The development of literacy skills thus remains connected to, and in the service of, the goals of the individual and the settings in which he or she lives, pursues leisure activities, goes to school, works, etc.

Methods

The specific methods for teaching literacy skills are numerous.[24] Some educators have stressed the usefulness of structured methods in teaching literacy skills, methods that begin with texts prescribed by the teacher and emphasize a "phonics" approach to learning to read. Others have emphasized beginning with a "language experience" approach that involves the learner in telling stories from personal experience. When transcribed by a tutor or educator, these become the texts used for learning to read. Specific methods for learning to read may include the development of a vocabulary of "sight words," words the individual learner finds in everyday life on signs and labels. This has been found to be an effective method when an individual is first learning to read and write. Flash cards, making and using labels, writing stories, reading in pairs, are all methods which literacy educators have used to assist learners.

Educators who were interviewed indicated that the effectiveness of any particular method depends on the individual, his or her goals for developing literacy, and the specific literacy requirements for achieving the goals. Adult learners made the same point. As one woman said:

> [After I left the institution] I started going to school, but I was starting at square one. I started in a class with fifteen other students. I tried sitting in the class, but I couldn't follow the method. It was too much. They had to read special books. The teacher was frustrated.

Maybe if she was in my shoes she would have a different sense of feeling... I was in a class with people who had failed their grades. I felt like I was left out, they were more advanced than me. To me that made a big difference, to have some schooling. I felt bad, I was embarassed.

So I started going to a lady's home for help, by myself. It took two years before I felt like I was reading and writing, *two* years. I went two nights a week and studied at home. I was working during the day at the workshop and going to classes at night.

There are no methods that are universally effective. Those that work for an individual learner, in light of his or her goals and needs for literacy, and the task requirements associated with these goals, become effective methods.

Monitoring and assessment

Another step in developing effective learning strategies involves monitoring of the learning process and assessing the literacy skills gained or still required. The research cited above on learning and mental handicap, as well as the research on literacy education, suggests that self-monitoring is essential for effective learning strategies. By reflecting on the strategies used, educators and learners can revise learning strategies and make them more able to achieve the learner's goals. Monitoring and assessment can address the nature of the goals that have been identified, the ways in which the task requirements have been formulated, and the specific methods chosen for learning literacy skills.

If individuals are not able to monitor or reflect on their own learning process, they are less able to make adjustments to the process to better suit their particular learning needs. A few of the educators who were interviewed identified self-monitoring as a challenge for some learners, and for educators. They felt that some individuals with a mental handicap tend to have greater difficulty or have fewer opportunities for reflecting on how they learn. One literacy educator who was interviewed said:

We don't know very well the language about learning...
[We do know that] people who haven't learned to talk
about their own learning have difficulty identifying
their weak areas and strong areas around learning.
When they can [talk about their own learning] then
they can set goals, and they can gauge their own progress.

Lytle suggests that in literacy education monitoring
should be ongoing. She stresses that the purpose of assessment
should not be to measure levels of "skill" against some fixed
standard of literacy. Instead, assessment should explore "the
particular types of reading and writing which adults themselves
see as meaningful under different circumstances and which
reflect their own needs and aspirations."[25] This approach involves learners in describing their own literacy practices and
strategies, and in assessing their effectiveness in light of personal goals.

A number of key points have been made in this chapter
about the relationship between learning, literacy, and mental
handicap. The analysis began with questioning the assumption
that individuals with a mental handicap have lower levels of
literacy because they posess inherent "deficits" that preclude
this possibility. Research and the experience of some individuals
and educators suggests that this assumption is unfounded. Individuals with a mental handicap can and do develop literacy
skills. Lower levels of literacy can be attributed more to the
tendency for adults with a mental handicap to lack effective
learning strategies or to use ineffective ones than to the presence
of a mental handicap. The lack of or use of ineffective learning
strategies is due to two major factors. Often adults with a mental handicap have been made dependent in many aspects of their
lives. To learn effectively, however, individuals must be able to
exercise some control over the learning process: over what will be
learned, how it will be learned, and with whom it will be learned.
One challenge for literacy education, and for literacy educators,
is to help break the "cycle of dependency" in which many adults
with a mental handicap are caught. Instructional approaches

that promote and enable some autonomy in the learning process are thus required.

Notes

[1]Thomas L. Whitman, "Self-Regulation and Mental Retardation," *American Journal on Mental Retardation*, Vol. 94, No. 4 (1990): p. 348.

[2]*Ibid.*

[3]See J.C. Campione and A.L. Brown, "Memory and metamemory development in educable retarded children," In R.V. Kail and J.W. Hagen (Eds.), *Perspectives on the development of memory and cognition* (Hillsdale, N.J.: Lawrence Erlbaum Associates, 1977).

[4]See, for example, David S. Katims and Ronnie N. Alexander, "Cognitive Strategy Training: Implications, Applications, Limitations," Paper presented at the Annual convention of the Council for Exceptional Children (Chicago, April 20-24, 1987).

[5]*Ibid.* For a discussion of the centrality of learning strategies to understanding "reading disability" see Peter H. Johnston, "Understanding Reading Disability: A Case Study Approach," *Harvard Educational Review*, Vol. 55, No. 2(1985): 153-177.

[6]For examples, see Whitman, "Self-Regulation and Mental Retardation."; James E. Martin and Dennis Mithaug, "Advancing a Technology of Self-Control," *B.C. Journal of Special Education*, Vol. 10, No. 2 (1986): 93-99.; Norman W. Bray and Lisa Turner, "Production Anomalies (Not Strategic Deficiencies) in Mentally Retarded Individuals," *Intelligence*, 11 (1987): 49-60;

[7]Katims and Alexander, "Cognitive Strategy Training: Implications, Applications, Limitations."

[8]H. Douglas Brown, *Principles of Language Learning and Teaching*, (Englewood Cliffs, New Jersey: Prentice-Hall, 1980), p. 83.

[9]Cited in James E. Turner, "Social Influences on Cognitivie Strategies and Cognitive Development: The Role of Communication and Instruction," *Intelligence*, 11 (1987), p. 78.

[10]For a general discussion of learning strategies see H. Douglas Brown, *Principles of Language Learning*, (Englewood Cliffs, New Jersey: Prentice-Hall, 1980). An overview of research on learning strategies, reading, and mental handicap is provided in L.P. Blanton, M.I. Semmel, and S.S. Rhodes, "Research on the reading of mildly mentally retarded learners: a synthesis of the empirical literature," in Sheldon Rosenberg (ed.), *Advances in applied psycholinguistics, Volume 2: Reading, writing and language learning,* (Cambridge: Cambridge University Press, 1987). Methods for developing learning strategies in literacy education with adults with a mental handicap is provided in The Scottish Community Education Council, *Moving Ahead: A new handbook for tutors helping mentally handicapped adults to learn.*

[11]E. Shapiro, "Self-control procedures with the mentally retarded," In M. Hersen, R. Eisler, and P. Miller (Eds.), *Progress in Behaviour Modification*, Vol. 12, (New York: Academic Press, 1981).

[12]Whitman, "Self-Regulation and Mental Retardation."

[13]James E. Martin and Dennis Mithaug, "Advancing an Technology of Self-Control," *B.C. Journal of Special Education*, Vol. 10, No. 2 (1986): 93-99.

[14]*Ibid.*

[15]B.W. Gottlieb, "Social facilitation influences on the oral reading performance of academically handicapped children," *American Journal of Mental Deficiency*, 87 (1982): 153-158.

[16]Marsha Forest, *It's About Learning,* (Toronto: Frontier College Press, 1988), p. 116.

[17]Whitman, "Self-Regulation and Mental Retardation," p. 360.

[18]Louise Doré, "On n'apprend pas à nager dans un bain," *Alpha Liaison,* vol. VII, no. 1 (oct. 1986): 19-22.

[19]Louise Doré, *Des gens comme vous et moi,* (Montreal: Editions coopératives St. Martin, 1982).

[20]J.C. Campione, "Metacognitive components of instructional re-search with problem learners," In F.E. Weinert and R.H. Kluwe (Eds.), *Metacognition, motivation, and understanding* (Hillsdale, New Jersey: Lawrence Erlbaum Associates, 1987).

[21]Norman W. Bray and Lisa A. Turner, "Production Anomalies (Not Strategic Deficiencies) in Mentally Retarded Individuals," *Intelligence* 11 (1987): pp. 56.

[22]Carpenter, *The Right to Read*, p. 33.

[23]Susan Lytle, "From the Inside Out: Reinventing Assessment," *Focus on Basics*, Vol. 2, No. 1 (Fall 1988), p. 3.

[24]See Carpenter, *The Right to Read*, for a good description of a variety of methods in teaching literacy skills to adults.

[25]See Lytle, "From the Inside Out: Reinventing Assessment," p. 3.

CHAPTER 5

FUNDING AND DELIVERY OF LITERACY EDUCATION

Adults with a mental handicap encounter a number of barriers to literacy. These barriers are examined in the following chapter. The barriers cannot be analyzed, however, without an understanding of the arrangements for funding and delivery of literacy education in Canada. This chapter outlines these arrangements. The purpose is not to provide a detailed description, but rather to present a general overview.

A variety of government initiatives and programs have evolved in Canada for the funding and support of literacy education. Delivery of literacy education has generally fallen within the broader policy and program framework of "adult basic education" (ABE). Although it is defined in a number of ways, ABE generally encompasses basic literacy education, academic upgrading, English as a second language training (ESL), and "mother-tongue" literacy programs. Provinces and territories generally provide this range of basic education services. Within an ABE policy and program framework, literacy training is often considered to be the first level of education and is directed to those adults who have not had formal schooling, whose grade level attainment is below the grade 5-7 range, or who require ESL training.

A number of non-governmental organizations, unions, and businesses are also involved in advocacy for, and funding and delivery of, literacy education. Each province/territory has at least one provincial non-governmental organization that serves

54

to provide resources, mobilize support, and promote awareness about literacy issues. It has become common in recent years to refer to these other actors as "partners" in literacy education. While these actors play an essential role in promoting literacy, the primary purpose in this chapter is to outline the policy framework for literacy education. The focus in the following discussion, therefore, is on the role of government.

DELIVERY OF LITERACY EDUCATION

Constitutionally, provincial and territorial governments have primary responsibility for education and consequently for funding and support of adult basic education and literacy education. To date, provincial and territorial levels of government have implemented funding arrangements for delivery of literacy programs and for financial support of learners outside of an explict and integrated policy framework for literacy education. In some cases, provinces and territories have designated a particular department or ministry to be primarily responsible for literacy education. These are sometimes called the "lead" department or ministry. Funding and supports for literacy education often cut across a number of departments including those concerned with education, advanced and post-secondary education and training, income assistance and social services, and economic development. Delivery mechanisms used in the provinces and territories for delivery of literacy education include:

- Community-based volunteer tutor programs
- Library programs
- Community college and training institutions
- School board and school district programs
- Work-based literacy programs

Provinces and territories vary substantially in the use of these mechanisms. A general description of each is provided below.

Community-based volunteer tutor programs

These programs are provided by a number of groups and agencies in the community. The setting for such programs may be community halls, churches, local schools, and a learner's home. The model provides for a program coordinator responsible for administration of a literacy project, for recruiting volunteer tutors, for training and support of tutors, and for acquisition of materials. Volunteer tutors work one-to-one with individuals and sometimes in small groups. They may operate completely autonomously, may be supported by a community college or school board, or by an umbrella organization such as Frontier College or Laubach Literacy. Programs are often funded through grants from a provincial or territorial government. Where a program is developed for purposes of demonstration the funding may be cost-shared through Secretary of State. Provincial/territorial governments either directly, or through colleges and school boards, may also support these initiatives through training events, information sharing, and provision of materials.

Library programs

Libraries also provide a setting for the delivery of literacy education. They are more likely to use literacy coordinators and educators employed or contracted by the library. Instruction is on a one-to-one and small group basis. School boards and community colleges may also contract libraries for the delivery of programs.

Community colleges and vocational training institutions

Community colleges and vocational training institutions are funded through grants from their respective provincial/territorial government, and by the federal and provincial/territorial governments through direct purchase of training courses and seats. Colleges generally provide both full- and part-time adult basic education courses. In some jurisdictions, colleges report directly to a minister of the provincial government and in other jurisdictions are autonomous bodies. A variety of programs are usually provided, including basic skills education, academic upgrading for all grade levels, vocational training that may include an academic or literacy component, and in some instances adult special education programs for adults with a disability.

Community colleges have also played an outreach role among various groups in the community. In some cases, they may facilitate the development of volunteer tutor programs, assist in coordination among various providers, and provide materials and training supports. As well, some colleges contract community-based groups, agencies, school boards, and libraries to deliver adult education programs.

Certain colleges within some jurisdictions have implemented support and counselling services for adults with a disability. These services include educational and vocational counselling, study groups, special tutors, equipment, and aides.

School board programs
In some jurisdictions, school boards deliver literacy-related education, both academic upgrading and literacy education through classroom-based instruction for adults. School boards have also acted as delivery agents for adult basic education services contracted by community colleges. In addition, some school boards provide outreach services to recruit learners who want to develop literacy skills and to support community-based volunteer tutor programs. Through their adult basic education programs some school boards have undertaken the development of curriculum and materials, and training events.

Work-based literacy
In some instances, work-based literacy education is offered through employment programs on the work-site and through unions or employers off the work-site. Because so few adults with a mental handicap participate in the paid labour force, this alternative has not been examined in this study. As more individuals with a mental handicap enter the workforce issues of availability and access to such work-based literacy programs will become increasingly important.

THE ROLE OF PROVINCIAL AND TERRITORIAL GOVERNMENTS

The role of provincial and territorial governments in the funding and delivery of literacy education is presented below.

British Columbia

While it has not been given a formal mandate as a lead ministry, the Ministry of Advanced Education, Training and Technology has primary responsibility for funding literacy education in British Columbia. Delivery is provided through the province's fifteen community colleges as well as through twenty of the seventy-five school districts.

The community colleges provide basic education and academic upgrading in more than one hundred locations throughout the province. The colleges are autonomous from government. Each college has staff positions for the coordination of literacy education and for the counselling and support of students with a disability. Because of their autonomy, the colleges have some flexibility in the design of their own programs. Generally, programs are provided on and off campus using a variety of modes of instruction including classroom-based and one-to-one instruction. Colleges have supported other community agencies in the delivery of literacy education, including volunteer tutor programs.

School districts provide evening and part-time basic education and academic upgrading. As well, school district adult completion programs are provided on a full-time basis through high schools. School districts also support and contract a variety of community agencies in the delivery of literacy education.

The Adult Literacy Contact Centre in Vancouver has been established as a clearinghouse and referral service for literacy education in British Columbia. It is jointly funded by the federal and provincial governments. It provides a toll-free province-wide number, refers callers to programs, and publishes a directory of basic education programs, a newsletter, and promotional materials on literacy.

58

Alberta

Funding for literacy education in Alberta is provided through Alberta Education, Alberta Advanced Education, and Alberta Career Development and Employment. A total of eleven community colleges and four Alberta Vocational Centres (for educationally disadvantaged adults) provide some form of adult basic education. Designated counsellors are provided at the community colleges for students with a disability.

Alberta Education provides funding to school districts for adult basic education programs. School districts contract Community Colleges to deliver some of these programs. Adult basic education is provided according to grade level criteria for grades 1-9. Programs must be sponsored by a school board and certified teachers must provide instruction.

Alberta Advanced Education funds fifty-five community-based "Volunteer Tutor Projects" (VTPs). VTPs must be sponsored by a Further Education Council, a council made up of representatives of the community. Funding from the department usually covers overhead costs and salaries of program coordinators. It also provides some funding to Further Education Councils to carry out needs assessment. The department provides base funding for academic upgrading provided through Alberta Vocational Centres. Programs delivered through Vocational Centres can only serve adults who have been identified as disadvantaged.

Through its Vocational Training Program, the department of Career Development and Employment funds basic education programs and provides financial assistance to students. It sponsors programs delivered through private institutions, industry, community organizations, and Alberta Vocational Centres. Programs must be less than one year in duration, serve those who are educationally or employment disadvantaged, and be oriented toward enhancing employability.

Transitional Vocational Programs offered through some Alberta Vocational Centres and community colleges provide opportunities for some adults with a "mild" mental handicap to obtain adult education. The programs are forty weeks in length with thirteen weeks of classroom instruction and twenty-seven weeks of work experience, with follow-up on-the-job support provided by community agencies.

Saskatchewan

The lead ministry for literacy education in Saskatchewan is the Ministry of Education. Literacy education is provided in Saskatchewan through colleges, the Saskatchewan Institute of Applied Science and Technology, public libraries, and community-based volunteer groups. Colleges have provided literacy programs on a full- and part-time basis. Literacy education is also delivered in night classes, day classes and at drop-in learning centres.

Some colleges provide adult special education programs for adults with a disability, and some, as well, provide support services including special tutors, aids, equipment, counselling, and referral.

In 1987, the Saskatchewan Literacy Council was established and mandated by the Premier and the Minister of Education to implement a community-based volunteer literacy strategy; to promote awareness of literacy issues; and to encourage initiatives by the corporate and public sectors.

Manitoba

The Ministry of Education is the lead ministry for literacy and basic education in Manitoba. The Ministry's Adult and Continuing Education Branch is responsible for development, implementation, coordination, funding, and monitoring of initiatives in adult basic education, English as a second language training, adult literacy, and adult special education. The Continuing Education Unit of this branch works with school divisions and community groups to deliver a variety of programming alternatives.

Manitoba's three community colleges also provide adult basic education through programs on campuses, in regional centres, and in communities across the province.

Ontario

In 1986, the provincial government announced a plan for adult basic literacy that focused on literacy for native groups, people with disabilities, those who are unemployed, older adults, persons involved with the correctional system, and women. The Ministries of Education, Skills Development, Colleges and Universities, Correctional Services, and Culture and Communications have some involvement in the delivery of literacy education.

In 1987, the Ministry of Skills Development was designated as the lead ministry for adult basic literacy. Through the Ontario Basic Skills Program, the Ministry funds basic education and skills training programs that are delivered through colleges of applied arts and technology. Colleges may also work with community-based groups in the delivery of programs. Ontario Community Literacy Grants are provided for the delivery of community-based literacy programs, materials development, and for research and demonstration/pilot projects. An Ontario Basic Skills in the Workplace Program provides funding for workplace literacy and skills development programs.

The Ministry of Education provides adult basic literacy and English as a second language training through school boards. School boards, colleges, libraries, and community groups may co-sponsor programs. One-to-one tutoring, small classes, part-time and evening, and adult day school programs are provided.

The Ministry of Colleges and Universities provides basic education, basic training, basic employment training, and job readiness training. The college-based programs are generally considered to be for more advanced students. The Ministry of Correctional Services provides literacy-related programs in correctional centres and detention centres. School boards and volunteers are involved. The Ministry of Culture and Communications provides project grants to libraries to improve accessibility and to acquire literacy materials and computer software for computer-assisted learning.

In 1989, provincial and federal funds were allocated to provide a literacy and language training resource centre in Toronto.

Quebec

The lead ministry for literacy education in Quebec is the Ministére de l'Éducation (MEQ). Within the Ministry, the responsible branch is Direction générale de l'Éducation des adultes. In 1982, the Jean Commission, after a review of adult education in the province, recommended that a campaign be mounted to address the needs for literacy.[1] In 1985, the MEQ began to fund school boards for the purpose of delivering literacy education. Adults, including those identified as having a "mild" handicap, can gain access to these literacy programs. Depending on the school board, literacy programs may be integrated or segregated for adults with a mild mental handicap. In 1987, the MEQ produced curriculum guidelines for the provision of literacy through the school boards. The Ministére de la santé et des services sociaux (Ministry of Health and Social Services) can also request local school boards to second teachers for the provision of literacy training in rehabilitation centres. The MEQ also funds popular education groups to deliver community-based programs.

New Brunswick

The Departments of Education and of Advanced Education and Training are involved in the funding and delivery of literacy education in New Brunswick. The Department of Education provides academic upgrading for adults who have not reached their twenty-first birthday. For those adults with very limited literacy skills "special education" programs are offered in both English language and French language schools.

The Ministry of Advanced Education and Training provides funding for the province's nine community colleges. Each college employs a literacy coordinator and literacy instructors who teach adult basic education classes to groups of four to eight learners. The Ministry also offers part-time night school programs in basic education and academic upgrading through the colleges.

Community-based volunteer tutor programs are delivered through local literacy councils funded by annual grants from the Department of Advanced Education and Training. Funding is delivered through the community colleges to the councils. The councils maintain liaison with, and receive support from, the colleges' literacy coordinators in the form of consultation and resources. The English language councils are associated with Laubach Literacy of New Brunswick, and the French language councils are associated with La Fédération d'alphabétisation du Nouveau-Brunswick.

The Ministry also funds, through cost-sharing arrangements under the federal-provincial Youth Strategy, five storefront learning centres in the province. The centres provide basic skills and computer skills training to individuals in the fifteen to twenty-four age group who have reading, writing, and math skills below the grade 9 level.

Nova Scotia

The Department of Education is responsible for adult education in Nova Scotia. Basic education programs are provided through some college campuses. The primary delivery agent is the twenty-one school boards in the province who provide adult basic education and academic upgrading. The colleges also provide some basic education programs.

Local literacy councils were established in the 1970s. There are now twenty councils across the province that are supported by Laubach Literacy. No core funding is provided by government. The Department of Advanced Education and Job Training provides educational materials for the tutoring programs delivered by these councils, as well as training and development for tutors. The community colleges, through college resource centres, make literacy education materials accessible to tutors.

The Nova Scotia Public Libraries also provide literacy education both in classes and through tutoring.

Prince Edward Island

The Departments of Industry and of Education are involved in delivery of adult basic education in Prince Edward Island. The Human Resource Development Division of the Department of Industry provides operating grants and materials to the three local Laubach literacy councils in the province. These councils recruit and train volunteer tutors to work with adult learners. An Adult Night Class Program, funded by the province and delivered by Holland College, provides part-time night classes free-of-charge to residents of the province who are eighteen years old and over. The College also supports literacy councils by providing access to resource centres.

Newfoundland
The Ministry of Education is the lead ministry responsible for literacy education in Newfoundland. The Ministry provides support, funding, and program guidelines for delivery of the lower levels of adult basic education. Programs are delivered by the province's five community colleges through full- and part-time programs. Each of the colleges has adult basic education and literacy coordinators.

There is a provincial Laubach Council and fourteen local councils, as well as a small number of other community-based volunteer tutor programs. There is no direct funding from the province for the volunteer tutor programs coordinated by the local literacy councils. The province does make a contribution through the provision of funding for a Laubach field worker who provides program support.

Northwest Territories
The Department of Education is the lead ministry responsible for adult basic education in the Northwest Territories. Literacy education in the N.W.T. is mandated to take into account a number of factors: only five of sixty communities in the N.W.T. are accessible by road; the majority of the population is made up of aboriginal peoples; and there are eight official languages including English, Inuktitut, Slavey, and five Dene languages. A Literacy Strategy intended to address the high rates of English illiteracy in the N.W.T. was implemented in 1989. Documents for a literacy policy that will guide a five-year literacy strategy are expected to be made public in the near future.

The primary delivery agency for adult basic education is Arctic College with six regional campuses and a number of learning centres located in communities throughout the N.W.T. The college offers basic education, academic upgrading and pre-vocational training. It maintains a network of more than forty adult educators who have responsibility for delivering adult education at the community learning centres. Adult educators work with local education authorities to identify adult education needs and to initiate programs.

The Ministry also provides grants and contributions to community-based volunteer tutor and paid tutor programs to assess needs for literacy and to deliver programs. Costs of coordinators, tutors, and materials are covered.

Local education authorities are not involved in the direct delivery of adult literacy education.

Yukon

The Ministry of Education is the lead ministry for literacy education in Yukon Territory. It provides funding to Yukon College for basic education and academic upgrading. Programs are delivered through a central campus in Whitehorse, and through twelve regional campuses.

The Ministry also provides funding to the Yukon Literacy Council. The Council receives core funding from the Ministry for two staff positions and overhead. It offers literacy classes, and recruits and trains volunteers for one-to-one tutoring.

THE ROLE OF THE FEDERAL GOVERNMENT

Because literacy is seen to be critical to economic and social development and to the availability of a skilled labour force, the federal government has played a financial and support role in literacy education. A number of federal departments are involved. Employment and Immigration Canada has, in the past, been involved in literacy-related education when it provided significant funding for purchase of "basic training for skill development" (BTSD), delivered through private agencies and employers, and through colleges and training institutions regulated by the provincial governments. These programs provided literacy-related education in the form of preparatory training in mathematics, sciences, reading, and communication skills. In 1970-71, 40 percent of all the training days purchased by the federal government were for BTSD. By 1983-84, this figure had declined to 12 percent.[2] From the mid-1970s on, the emphasis in the purchase of training shifted from basic education to the development of occupationally-specific skills identified through the analysis of future labour needs of the economy.

Under the Canadian Jobs Strategy (CJS), the department will now purchase "preparation for vocational training," a purchasing option that has essentially replaced BTSD and other job entry programs (Basic Job Readiness Training, and Job Readiness Training). It is intended to be focused more directly on preparation for further skill training related to a specific occupational goal. However, eligibility criteria for the program specifies that it is for the purchase only of academic upgrading above grade 7. The criteria exclude, therefore, individuals who have grade level or academic achievement below grade 7, and who do not have a specific occupational goal. Through the CJS job entry and job development programs, funding has been allocated for "on-the-job" training of literacy tutors, thereby indirectly supporting delivery of literacy education. This has provided the opportunity for some community organizations to develop or extend literacy education. However, the program criteria allow a maximum duration of fifty-two weeks. Programs based solely on these funding arrangements lack a stable funding base. For individuals, including those with a mental handicap, who participate in CJS job development and job entry programs, a maximum of three weeks classroom-based or tutor-based education is normally allowable. Only a short period of time is allowed because the emphasis is on on-the-job training.

Through the Secretary of State, the federal government has articulated an overall policy on literacy. In its 1986 Speech from the Throne, the federal government made a commitment to working on literacy initiatives with other levels of government, private business, the non-governmental organizations and voluntary sectors, and labour organizations. The purpose of the policy is to enable adults in Canada to have the opportunity to develop their literacy skills. In 1987, the Secretary of State announced the establishment of the National Literacy Secretariat and in 1988 the National Literacy Program was announced. More than $100 million was allocated for cost-shared literacy initiatives with the provinces and territories. Funding is allocated to projects to develop learning materials, to support demonstration projects, to improve access and outreach programs, to improve information sharing and coordination in delivery and program support, and to increase public awareness. Under the National Literacy Program, federal funds are not allocated for direct delivery of literacy education, and all projects must be cost-shared.

Correctional Services of Canada, of the federal Ministry of the Solicitor General, also provides funding for literacy education within correctional facilities under the jurisdiction of the federal government.

This chapter has provided an overview of the arrangements for funding and delivery of literacy education in Canada. There are a variety of arrangements, and numerous programs. We know very little, however, about the numbers of adults with a mental handicap who participate in these programs. One clear conclusion can be drawn from the analysis and interviews carried out for this study: adults with a mental handicap have negligible access to literacy education. The following chapter examines the barriers to literacy encountered by adults with a mental handicap.

Notes

[1]Commission d'étude sur la formation des adultes (Commission Jean), *Apprendre: une action volontaire et responsable*, (Quebec: Ministère des communications, 1982).

[2]See Annual Reports of what is now known as Department of Employment and Immigration. In the 1970s the Department was named Manpower and Immigration. The Annual Reports reviewed began with the Report for 1970/71.

CHAPTER 6

BARRIERS TO LITERACY

Adults with a mental handicap gain access to literacy education in very small numbers. For many at present, the barriers to literacy are insurmountable. While a more detailed analysis of these barriers awaits further research, this study identifies them and provides an initial analysis. The barriers to literacy education for adults with a mental handicap include:

- attitudinal barriers
- policy and program barriers to participation
- barriers to learning

Three terms are used in this chapter to refer to those who are involved in the delivery of literacy education. *Program coordinators* refer to those individuals responsible for program development, administration, training, development, and ongoing support of literacy educators and tutors involved in a program. The term *educator* is used to refer to a paid literacy educator within a program, whether at a college, school board, library, or other community-based program. The term *tutor* is used to refer to volunteers who assist adult learners in developing their literacy skills. Volunteer tutors are usually involved in community-based volunteer programs. These are not mutually exclusive distinctions. Where the term *educator* is used below it often encompasses program coordinators and tutors, both of whom also act as educators.

ATTITUDINAL BARRIERS

As indicated in the previous chapter, the experience of many individuals is that once they are labelled "mentally handicapped," others in the community question their capacity to learn. This means their capacity to develop literacy skills is also put into question. The story of one woman who wanted to gain access to a community literacy program makes the point clear. In an interview, her mother explained:

> Brenda wanted to do some more work on her reading and writing. When she was originally at school, the teachers were very good and Brenda began to read and write. So I heard about a community program for literacy for adults and gave them a call. They gave me information about the program, it sounded fine, so we agreed to meet. Well, when we arrived and sat down, they saw Brenda's face for the first time, and saw that she has "Down's." They said then that it simply wasn't possible. She wouldn't be able to attend the program.

Adult learners who were interviewed for this study also indicated that while they believed in their own capacity to learn, others did not always share this view. One man interviewed for the study said:

> When I was in school the teacher thought I was a retarded person and couldn't learn how to read. So she made me go to work with a bunch of handicapped children where all I did was change dirty diapers and clean vomit up off the floor.
>
> At night school Miss Harriet said I couldn't learn what I wanted to. Everytime I wanted to learn something she said, "No, you have to learn what I want you to learn."
>
> When I went through that I would wake up with nightmares. I was so scared by my teachers. They would say, "You're not going to amount to anything, you'll just be

a fat retarded person." And I said, "My dear woman, you're wrong." And I decided I just had to learn to read because if I don't then the teacher will have been right.

A woman recounted:

> I lived in an institution for fourteen years. If you've never gone to school you were never taught how to read and write... The doctors in the institution thought I could never learn. They never gave me the opportunity. They never gave me the chance. Sometimes professionals criticize too much. I said to myself if you're going to be independent you're going to have to learn to read and write... It's an awful thing when you're forgotten about.

Another woman said:

> I left school after grade 6. I was in special classes but what could you do. What confused me is they send you around to different schools and then you're really confused. I blame my social worker... The social worker pulled me out and put me in a workshop. They said that I couldn't learn anything. It was their word against mine. They said, "It wouldn't have done you any good"... I don't want a social worker calling. She thinks she knows more than me. They sort of try to run your life. It's not my fault that I've been labelled. They're not giving you the opportunity... I was in the workshop for eleven years, cuttin' lumber and unloading trailers. The staff, they try to tell you things to do and you don't want to do them. They think you're stupid...

There are four points at which adults with a mental handicap encounter other individuals whose attitudinal barriers may limit their access to literacy education:

- those who provide vocational and educational counselling, assessment, and referral;

- those who make decisions with respect to funding and training allowances for individuals;

- counsellors and support workers employed by residential and vocational service agencies; and,

- providers of literacy education.

Vocational and educational counselling, assessment, and referral are provided through a number of mechanisms. Vocational counsellors employed or contracted by the provincial or territorial governments assist individuals in planning for and obtaining vocational training and other employment-related supports funded through federal-provincial cost-sharing arrangements and other provincial funding sources.[1] Social workers or caseworkers employed or contracted by the provincial or territorial governments may also play a role in determining the educational opportunities in which an adult who is on social assistance may participate. Employment counsellors with local Canada Employment Centres, or with agents contracted by Employment and Immigration Canada (EIC), also play a counselling and assessment role. They provide these services both for Unemployment Insurance claimants who wish to enroll in training and educational activities, and for those who are not claimants, but who wish to obtain training allowances to participate in EIC-funded training. Individuals in these positions not only provide counselling, assessment, and referral services, but they may also make recommendations about, or approve, the funding and training allowances individuals will receive. Providers of literacy education whether at a community college, school board, library, or community-based volunteer tutor program also present attitudinal barriers that limit access to literacy education.

Individuals in all of these positions have, to a greater or lesser degree, the discretionary power to make decisions about the training and education opportunities that will be available to adults with a mental handicap. Their discretionary power, however, is not the problem. Rather, it is often that because of their attitudes and assumptions about the limited learning capacity of adults with a mental handicap they use their discretionary power in ways that limit access to literacy education. Throughout the interviews conducted for this study the following reasons were cited for the use of discretionary power to limit rather than enable access to literacy education.

First, those with discretionary decision-making power often assume that adults with a mental handicap cannot adequately learn or develop literacy skills: the fact that they have a mental handicap is assumed to preclude these possibilities. As a result, literacy education may simply not be presented or considered as an option by those in counselling and referral positions. Based on this assumption, literacy providers have also refused access to literacy programs.

Second, it has been assumed that adults with a mental handicap will not be able to keep up with the pace of basic education or academic upgrading courses. Adult learners, as well, said that the pace of classroom-based adult education and academic upgrading is often delivered in a manner that is inaccessible to them. The problem, however, is seen to reside with the adult learner, and not with the inflexibility of the program.

Third, the process of learning literacy skills often proceeds at a much slower pace for adults with a mental handicap than for other adults. This creates two problems. The first is that adults often require training allowances to meet their living costs while in literacy-related education. The time-limits set on the allowances are often too short, however, for adults with a mental handicap to remain in the program long enough to adequately develop literacy skills. The second problem is that the program itself may have time limits that are insufficient for the learning needs of adults with a mental handicap. Again, the result is an assumption that the problem lies with the individual, who is seen to be incapable of learning, rather than the characteristics inherent in the income support system or the literacy program.

Fourth, those with decision-making power often assume that the majority of adults with a mental handicap will *plateau* in their level of learning at a grade 3 or 4 academic level. Investment in academic upgrading beyond this level is questioned on the grounds that substantial advances in learning will not be made beyond this level. As a result, they believe the program is not a viable option for adults.

Fifth, it was suggested that even if individuals do make some advances in their level of reading and writing, these advances are not likely to be sufficient to make an appreciable difference in the kinds of employment opportunities that will be open to them. Those who make decisions about allocating scarce dollars for vocational and employment-related training may, therefore, be reluctant to recommend literacy education as an option. Vocational training, which does not include extensive literacy education, is determined to be the preferred option.

Sixth, a concern has been expressed by some about the social stigma that an adult with a mental handicap may bring to a literacy program. A review of literacy education in the United Kingdom, for instance, found that adults who "visibly" had a mental handicap were less likely to obtain access to a community-based literacy program than those who "[look] normal, whatever their abilities."[2]

POLICY AND PROGRAM BARRIERS

In addition to attitudinal barriers to literacy education, there are a number of policy and program barriers related to delivery of literacy education. These include:

- program funding
- costs to the individual
- eligibility criteria
- supports and services
- outreach and linkage

Program funding

Funding for literacy programs is required to cover the cost of program coordinators, educators (where volunteer tutors are not used), educational materials, and overhead. Three aspects of program funding affect whether or not adults with a mental handicap have access to literacy education.

First, inadequate levels of program funding, whether for community-based literacy education or academic upgrading, has been found to be a general barrier to literacy education. This barrier affects both adults with a mental handicap and other adults. There is a widely acknowledged lack of resources for literacy education. This is due to limited funding and to a lack of educational materials in some settings.

Second, in addition to its impact on program availability, underfunding of literacy programs limits the capacity of programs to include adults with a mental handicap. Underfunded programs lack a sufficient number of paid coordinators to develop and provide support to tutors/educators. Higher levels of support tend to be required for tutors/educators of adults with a mental handicap because these adult learners present unique challenges. A dearth of paid program coordinators who provide back-up and support to tutors has restricted the numbers of tutors able and willing to work with adults with a mental handicap.

A third program funding issue concerns the way in which financial resources are allocated to the various kinds of vocational and educational programs for adults with a mental handicap. Generally, decisions have not been made at a program level to allocate resources to literacy education for this group. Many adults with a mental handicap who are on social assistance participate in some form of specialized life skills or vocational training. This training is "targetted" to adults with a mental handicap and is delivered by community service agencies, individuals, educational institutions and sometimes employers. Training is contracted by provincial governments and funded under provisions of the Canada Assistance Plan, federal-provincial/territorial agreements under the Vocational Rehabilitation of Disabled Persons Act; in some provinces, under separate provincial funding sources; and, under certain options of the Canadian Jobs Strategy for on-the-job training and time-limited supported employment. Training options include "sheltered workshops," day programs for the development of social and life skills, specialized vocational training programs for adults with a mental handicap delivered through community colleges or vocational training institutions, and on-the-job training and job coaching in a competitive employment setting. A few agencies have incorporated a literacy component into their sheltered workshop and training options. Some specialized vocational training programs delivered through community colleges or

74

vocational training institutes also include some instruction in reading and writing. However, this is usually not the primary focus of the program. On-the-job training may include a literacy component if individuals must learn to carry out specific reading and writing tasks as part of their job.

These programs represent the major set of vocational training programs in which adults with a mental handicap participate. While individuals may have access to some vocational and training opportunities, most often these programs do not include literacy education. Funding is generally allocated to the providers of the program, and, consequently, individuals do not have the financial means to go elsewhere to purchase literacy education should they choose to do so. And because the funds are targetted for training adults with a mental handicap, accessing additional funding allocations for literacy education can be difficult.

Costs to the individual

Costs to individuals also pose a barrier to their participation in literacy programs. Three kinds of costs are encountered: (1) the cost of the program; (2) the cost of participating in the program; and (3) the loss of income support.

Because most adults with a disability are poor, many lack the income that may be required to enroll in literacy education, adult basic education, or academic upgrading programs. While some of these programs are free, many are not. As well, some of those who were interviewed for this study indicated that even if literacy programs were free to the participant, costs of transportation and of attendant care or other personal support would be encountered. Without these supports many adults with a mental handicap are not able to participate.

Maintaining income support while participating in literacy programs has also been a difficulty for some adults. Because only 25 percent of adults with a mental handicap are in the paid labour force, most receive some form of social assistance. Rules for provision of social assistance vary from province to province. In some instances, these rules have prohibited adults with a mental handicap, as well as other adults, from participating in literacy education or other education/training opportunities while in receipt of social assistance.

As well, some of those who were interviewed indicated that adults who receive unemployment insurance have had difficulty in maintaining their benefits when they enroll in full-time literacy education. The recommendations of the Labour Force Development Strategy of Employment and Immigration Canada address this disincentive to some degree. It recommends that Unemployment Insurance benefits be provided to individuals while they obtain their secondary school equivalence, where this is required for participation in further training.[3] The problem with this recommendation is that it does not address the income support needs of those who have not been able to obtain basic education below the secondary level (the case for many adults with a mental handicap) but who still want to participate in literacy education.

Eligibility criteria
There are two types of eligibility criteria affecting participation in literacy programs by adults with a mental handicap: (1) those establishing required levels of academic achievement or of measured intelligence; and (2) those imposing time limitations for participation in literacy education. These criteria tend to be applied more in adult basic education and academic upgrading delivered by community colleges and school boards than in community-based volunteer tutor programs.

With respect to the achievement-oriented criteria, Employment and Immigration Canada, for example, uses the criterion of attainment of grade 7 for participation in the "preparation for vocational training" programs that it purchases and that are delivered by a community college or some other agent. Grade level attainment and scores on intelligence tests have also served as eligibility criteria for training and education in other programs delivered by community colleges and vocational training institutes. Because a number of adults with a mental handicap have not had the opportunity to proceed through the regular school system, they have not attained the grade levels or developed the related level of skills. Even where they have, there are significant reliability problems associated with measuring intelligence and with assessing grade levels. One educator interviewed indicated the "Test for Adult Basic Education" or TABE is a very unreliable measure of grade level. Individuals can test one day and achieve a grade 8 standing, and test the next day and receive a grade 6 standing. Neither is it apparent that the problem of unreliability is exclusive to the TABE test. This degree of unreliability has then the unfortunate potential to "make or break" an adult's educational opportunities.

One government official who was interviewed indicated a need for criteria to determine ongoing eligibility once an individual is enrolled in literacy education. It was considered that such criteria would address the issue of adults who do not seem, by some standards, to progress in adult basic education or academic upgrading programs at a sufficient rate. For policy makers concerned with how to allocate resources to literacy education this is a growing issue. Limited resources mean that adults who are not considered to be progressing at an adequate pace take up program seats that other adults may be able to use. Thus, some consideration has been given to the use of assessment tools that more systematically measure the pace at which individuals develop literacy skills. Those who do not meet required standards would be channelled into other pre-vocational or vocational training that require minimal or no literacy skills.

Time-limited criteria are used in basic education and academic up-grading programs, sometimes implicitly because of the duration of a program, and sometimes explicitly by limiting the number of hours an individual can participate in a program. These criteria are used in many school board and community college programs. As well, many of the pre-vocational and vocational training programs purchased by Employment and Immigration Canada that include a literacy-related component have a fifty-two-week limit. In some instances provincial governments have imposed or are considering the imposition of time-limited criteria for literacy education. In Quebec, for example, participation in literacy programs funded by the Ministère de l'Éducation and delivered through school boards is limited to 2,000 hours per student. Some of the people interviewed for this study indicated that this time limitation was not adequate for a significant number of adults with a mental handicap. For many adults, it can take up to six months just to get settled and accustomed to the program and the learning process. In Quebec, both achievement-oriented and time-limited eligibility criteria are combined to stream adults into and through literacy education. Providers of literacy education through school boards are required to separate adults with a "mild" mental handicap from adults with a "moderate" mental handicap. Only those designated as "mild" can attend the literacy program. Others with moderate or more "profound" handicaps may attend a program to develop skills for living in the community, a program that may include development of some minimal literacy skills.[4] The time limitation on this program is 1,920 hours.

Some of those interviewed indicated that the use of these criteria presented two problems. First, it was difficult to separate people with a "mild" mental handicap from those with a "moderate" handicap. In fact, this distinction, in itself draws on an assumption that adults with a mental handicap have fixed and unchanging intellectual deficits. The assumption leads to the conclusion that, depending on the level of deficit measured, individuals can be categorized into different levels or groups. Second, the use of these criteria meant that the needs and the interests of the learner were not the primary consideration in delivery of literacy education: those who may want to develop literacy skills but are labelled "moderate" are not eligible for the literacy program delivered through school boards. Third, the time limitation is not considered adequate for many adults with a mental handicap to develop their literacy skills.

Any program will inevitably have eligibility criteria. However, it can be argued that a principle of distributive justice should be used to guide the selection and design of such criteria: resources should be allocated in fair and just ways. In the area of literacy, the principles of a "right to literacy," "a right to education," and a "right to learning" for all adults are increasingly advocated as principles whose achievement is necessary to secure justice. However, it appears that on balance the kinds of eligibility criteria that are in place tend to exclude more than include adults with a mental handicap in literacy education that is effective for them.

Supports and services

Access to literacy education by adults with a mental handicap is
also affected by the need for, and access to, supports and services.
The need for support to participate in literacy education is made
even more complex when, in addition to a mental handicap,
adults also have sensory (visual, hearing), agility, or mobility
impairments. It is estimated that 19 percent of adults with a
mental handicap have hearing impairments; 28 percent have
visual impairments; and over 40 percent have some speech
difficulties. Approximately 40 percent are estimated to have
agility and/or mobility impairments.[5] For some individuals
access to literacy education is dependent on the provision of drug
therapies, attendant care and personal support, transportation,
and assistive devices and equipment.

According to some of the educators who were interviewed,
adults with a mental handicap, more than other adults, have
been placed on drug therapies that affect their cognitive functioning and behaviour and might potentially affect the learning
process. As one educator said, adults with a mental handicap
"are often heavily drugged and this factor impedes learning:
medication is the biggest stopper." It was also suggested that
drug therapies often appear to induce even greater "passivity"
than it is felt adult learners might otherwise demonstrate. In
some cases, it was maintained, the drug therapies served no
other purpose than to keep the individual in a passive state. And
in some instances, individuals in literacy programs have been
found to be taking a number of different medications prescribed
by different doctors for the same condition. While this problem
is too large to be resolved at the doors of literacy programs, the
research suggests that tutors and educators would benefit from:

- more information on drug therapies and their implications for
  cognitive and behavioural functioning;

- greater awareness about how to make appropriate interven-
  tions where there is a question or concern about the amount
  of medication taken by an individual, and/or the consequences
  of medication for the individual.

Adults who need attendant care or personal support are also faced with barriers to literacy education. First, funding for attendant care that the person needs to be able to participate in a literacy program is difficult, if not impossible to obtain. When funding for attendant care is available, it is usually only provided while an individual is in vocational training, employment, or in the home. Literacy or adult basic education is generally not considered as part of a "fundable" vocational plan for adults with a mental handicap. Second, even if restrictive conditions are not attached to the funding of attendant care, there is often very little flexibility in the times that attendants are available. As a result, it can be difficult to schedule attendant care around literacy classes or tutoring sessions. Even if attendant care or other personal supports can be arranged to enable participation in literacy education, access to literacy education is not ensured. Some programs have stipulated that unless individuals can participate in the program completely independently they will not be accommodated.

Adults who require transportation to participate in literacy education encounter a number of difficulties as well. In some cases, they cannot make use of the regular transportation system as a result of mobility impairments and/or the need to use a wheelchair. The specialized transit buses and vans for those with a mobility impairment often require bookings far in advance. If tutoring sessions have to be changed at the last minute because of conflicting schedules, it may not be possible to arrange transportation. As well, with more and more individuals using this system, bookings are becoming increasingly difficult to get. In smaller centres and rural areas, where these services are not available, transportation is an especially critical issue.

Those who require wheelchairs, other equipment, or communication assistive devices face further barriers to participating in literacy education. Obtaining funding for the purchase of these supports is subject to the same difficulties encountered by adults with a mental handicap in obtaining any funding for literacy education. As well, a recent study in Ontario found that programs are very often inaccessible to those with a physical disability. This is both because of physical barriers and because coordinators and educators are often reluctant to provide the necessary assistance for basic physical activities, such as eating and using the washroom.[6]

Outreach and linkage

The rate of participation in literacy education by adults with a mental handicap is very low. Outreach activities are a critical factor in increasing the participation of these adults in literacy education. With a few exceptions, there has not been an effort on the part of literacy educators to reach out to the community of adults with a mental handicap. It is suspected that in most instances an outreach strategy for this community has not been consciously considered. Neither, it appears, have Associations for Community Living (ACLs) or chapters of "People First," except in a few instances, actively sought links with literacy programs and educators to encourage participation in literacy education. A more active outreach and coordination effort, however, could not be accomplished or have an immediate impact without taking into account the various systematic barriers to literacy education discussed in this chapter.

BARRIERS TO LEARNING

Chapter Four outlined the features of an instructional approach to literacy education which has enabled adults with a mental handicap to learn literacy skills. These features constitute a "learner-centred" approach to literacy education. A learner-centred approach is increasingly stressed in the literacy literature as well as in government documents and proposals on literacy policy and delivery. This approach has evolved out of the "functional" conception of literacy, whereby individuals identify their own goals and needs. This information, gleaned through an initial informal assessment prior to an adult's participation in a program, becomes the basis for designing a program of literacy education around the individual. Those who were interviewed indicated that a learner-centred approach is most effective for adults with a mental handicap because it encourages them to take greater control of their own learning process.

A learner-centred approach also requires that the learning process be mutual. If tutors and educators are to be effective in realizing this approach, they must be able to learn from the adult learners themselves about their interests, goals, experience, and the barriers to learning that lie in other aspects of their lives.

This is particularly challenging for tutors and educators, in large part because of their assumptions about mental handicap, and adults who have been labelled in this way. However, as some of those who were interviewed indicated, it is essential that tutors and educators learn to respect the value, capacities, and potential of adults with a mental handicap. One tutor spoke about her experience in tutoring adults with a mental handicap:

> Learning happens within a relationship of dignity, understanding, respect of difference, and commitment to someone's goals. I'm learning about patience and dignity, what it's like to be labelled, and I'm inspired... Harold [an adult learner] teaches me. Now I'm open to his possibility.

A coordinator of a literacy program echoed this position and stated:

> When I think about what they have taught me... Gary came to the program all the time. After a year and a half he said, "I want to write about my father." He's nuts about his dad. His memories are very strong - he taught me a lot about parents, about parenting. When he finished telling me the story about his father he was crying. How can we value this less than a Ph.D? Gary's taught me how to value the fact that the disenfranchised have as much to say as those with a Ph.D. But it's a constant struggle.

There are a number of barriers to realizing a learner-centred approach to instruction and education for adults with a mental handicap. These barriers are related to:
- training and development of educators and tutors
- materials
- modes of instruction
- linkages

82

Training and development of educators and tutors

The need for training of educators and tutors was identified many times through the interviews as an important factor in enabling adults with a mental handicap to learn literacy skills. Many of those who were interviewed indicated that tutors and educators are often uncertain about how to assist an adult with a mental handicap in developing his or her literacy skills. They often lack confidence in their abilities when it comes to working with adults with a mental handicap; they may assume that adults with a mental handicap are not able to develop literacy skills, and they are sometimes fearful of working with adults who have been labelled in this way. One result is that volunteer tutors, for instance, are more difficult to find for adults with a mental handicap than for other adults. There was also a concern expressed by some program coordinators and government officials that it may be too much to ask of a volunteer to work with an adult with a mental handicap, given his or her "special" needs. One government official suggested that adults with a mental handicap should, as a result, be channelled away from community-based volunteer programs and into "institutional" (college-based, school board-based) literacy programs where there are paid, specially trained educators.

Those who have worked closely with adults with a mental handicap in literacy education suggested otherwise. They indicated that this group of adults does not need to be streamed into special programs, and that highly specialized educators are not required. While adults with a mental handicap are among the most challenging in a literacy program, they felt that all adults who have low levels of literacy skills have "special" needs. In other words, the "special" need is a lack of literacy not the mental handicap.

Those who were interviewed indicated that training and development strategies have not adequately addressed the concerns of tutors and educators. They often feel unprepared to deal with the needs and issues that adults with a mental handicap present. Commonly these include:

- a learning process that is often extremely slow in comparison to other adults;

- the reluctance of many adults with a mental handicap to articulate or develop a set of learning goals;

- the cognitive difficulties that may be encountered to a greater degree than with other adults (for example, probems with remembering, logic, drawing on past experiences to bring meaning to reading and writing);

- "behaviours" that seem threatening to tutors;

- the difficulty of verbal communication;

- the need because of a mobility impairment for assistance with eating or using the washroom;

- the behavioural and cognitive difficulties that may be induced by medications;

- the need by some adults for communication assistance technologies to develop their literacy skills. These technologies, involving computers and adaptive equipment, are foreign to some tutors and educators. Dealing with both the technologies and the development of literacy skills with someone who is not able to communicate verbally is extremely challenging;

- the fact that adults often present personal problems that tutors/educators do not always feel capable of addressing. These problems vary but include: "how to survive" in the community after leaving an institution, perceived discrimination in an individual's place of work, problems with family members or support staff at an individual's home, concerns about contracting sexually transmitted diseases, and personal and sexual relationships; and,

84

- whether, and to what extent, literacy educators and
  tutors should become involved in personal advocacy for
  adult learners who present personal problems to them.

While these issues present real challenges to literacy educators, many who were interviewed felt that with adequate training and development strategies, these challenges would be overcome.

Materials

This research found that if literacy education is to be more effective for adults with a mental handicap there is a need for materials both for adult learners and for educators.

For adult learners, materials for developing "functional" literacy skills are widely available depending on what an individual wants to learn. Educators and tutors use bus schedules, newspapers, labels from packaged foods and from medications etc. to develop literacy skills. They also develop their own materials. For example, flash cards and photographs are made to assist adults in learning "sight words" they encounter in their daily life. As skills develop, various texts and other resources are used. Reading and learning materials are often available through libraries, resource centres at community colleges, and through other arrangements established by the lead provincial/territorial ministries for adult literacy education.

The framework of "critical literacy" is useful in describing the kinds of materials that are currently lacking for adult learners with a mental handicap. First, materials are needed to change the standard for literacy, thereby making more usable the literacy skills that adults have or that they are able to develop. In other words, materials are needed that are written in plain and accessible language and that provide a range of information: for example, information about using the health care system; renting apartments; applying for various forms of income support; appealing decisions of government officials on benefits, allowances, and social assistance; rights and responsibilities in different contractual arrangements; and about using the legal aid system.

Second, materials that give expression to the experiences

of adults with a mental handicap are needed, materials that would give them a "voice." Some of the educators who were interviewed indicated that one of the biggest challenges to adults with a mental handicap who are beginning to read is finding meaning in written material. While individuals may be able to learn by "rote," maintenance of their reading skills is difficult if they cannot find meaning. Writing stories or letters that use words to communicate meaning is thus difficult as well. It was suggested by some educators that finding meaning in existing literature can be more difficult for adults with a mental handicap because many have not shared the experiences of other adults,— experiences that have usually been given expression in literature. These are experiences of growing up in the community, travelling, geography, politics, family relationships, school and university. The experiences known best by many adults with a mental handicap are those of living in an institution, being treated differently, struggling in the community, experiencing discrimination, and living in poverty and loneliness. Forms of literature written by and with adults with a mental handicap and literature about their own particular experience would be a valuable resource for literacy education. Some literacy programs encourage adult learners to begin their literacy education with their own stories, and some programs also provide facilities for publishing their work. There is room for further development in this direction.

Mode of instruction

Many of those who were interviewed suggested that literacy instruction needed to be made much more responsive to individual needs. Two important factors were identified: (1) the extent to which programs relied exclusively on classroom-based instruction; and (2) the opportunity for computer-assisted learning.

It was suggested by some of the self advocates and educators interviewed for this study that adults with a mental handicap tend to have more difficulty in literacy programs that are exclusively classroom-based. They learn more effectively, and more quickly, with one-to-one support. However, it was suggested that many literacy and basic education programs delivered by school boards and community colleges do not provide one-to-one support. Adults with a mental handicap have often been refused access to programs on the grounds that they will likely not benefit from exclusively classroom-based instruction. If accessibility to literacy education is to be increased, greater effort on the program delivery side will be required to respond to the individual's particular learning styles.

Some self advocates and educators who were interviewed indicated that computer-assisted learning can also enable literacy education to be more responsive to the learning needs of adults with a mental handicap. A variety of software programs are becoming available. Those interviewed suggested that the PALS and Pathfinder programs had been found by adults to be effective learning tools and to be enjoyable for adults to use. Computer-assisted learning was found to be effective for the following reasons:

- it allows adults to work on their own, mitigating the need for classroom involvement if this is not desired;

- it allows adults to work at their own speed;

- it is adaptable to the individual providing for various levels of both challenge and opportunities for success;

- it encourages adults to be self-correcting;

- it does not judge individuals; and,

- it provides an educator with a measure of the development of an adult's literacy skills, which can then be used for ongoing assessment.

Linkages
Effective linkage mechanisms are required to mitigate the barriers to learning that adults with a mental handicap face prior to, during, and beyond literacy education.

Linkage between literacy programs and other aspects of an adult's life was identified as an important factor in maximizing the learning for adults with a mental handicap. It was suggested by some that greater efforts were required (where an adult learner was willing) to work with support workers, family members, co-workers, and others involved in the adult's life. This would allow them, through an exchange of methods and strategies, to support the "literacy-learning" process whether at home, at work, or elsewhere.

Linkages between literacy programs and other education, training, and employment opportunities is also critical for adults with a mental handicap. Adults are likely to need support and assistance if they are to move beyond literacy education to other learning opportunities. Barriers they confront when seeking further education, training, or employment opportunities may be equally challenging. As well, without the links that expose adult learners to other viable opportunities, they may not be encouraged to move beyond the particular program to these other learning opportunities.

In summary, the barriers to literacy for adults with a mental handicap are extensive. Prevailing attitudes and assumptions about the learning capacity of adults with a mental handicap have operated to exclude access to literacy education. These assumptions have resulted in a "self-fulfilling prophecy." Adults with a mental handicap cannot gain access to literacy education because of the false assumption that they are not able to adequately learn and develop literacy skills. Without the opportunity, they are not able to develop literacy skills, and their tendency to have lower levels of literacy is misattributed to their mental handicap. The research suggests that a number of policies also pose barriers to participation in literacy education, including polices related to funding literacy programs, to eligibilty criteria for participation in programs, to individual income support to cover the cost of literacy education, and to provision of supports and services. At the level of program delivery, the barriers to participation include an inability or unwillingness on the part of providers to accommodate the needs of adults with a mental handicap. As well, inadequate outreach strategies by program providers have limited the potential for adults with a mental handicap to participate.

88

The chapter's final section examined those barriers to the process of learning encountered by adults. The research suggests that training and development strategies of educators and tutors have not taken into account the particular learning needs and issues that are presented by adults with a mental handicap in literacy education. Materials that are accessible to adults and that speak to their own experiences are also lacking. Modes of instruction to increase program responsiveness need wider implementation. Finally, the lack of program linkages, which maximize a range of learning opportunites, also pose barriers to learning.

Notes

[1]Federal-provincial cost-sharing arrangements of the *Vocational Rehabilitation of Disabled Persons Act* (VRDP) and other provincial funding sources enable provinces to provide funding for vocational training and as well as assessment, planning, counselling, and support services. The purpose of this funding is to assist individuals in obtaining training and employment.

[2]Adult Literacy and Basic Skills Unit, *Literacy and Numeracy Work with Mentally Handicapped Adults* (London: February 1982), p. 9.

[3]Employment and Immigration Canada, *Success in the Works: A Policy Paper. A Labour Force Development Strategy for Canada* (Ottawa: April 1989), p. 9.

[4]The program is titled "Programme d'insertion à la vie communautaire."

[5]These estimates are based on analysis of data from the Health and Activity Limitation Survey.

[6]See Jeffrey Freedman, *The Accessibility of Literacy Upgrading in the Community for Adults with Disabilities* (Toronto: Centre for Independent Living in Toronto, 1988).

CHAPTER 7

CURRENT POLICY PROPOSALS

This chapter briefly considers the kinds of recommendations for an explicit literacy policy that some provincial governments are being encouraged to adopt. The purpose of this chapter is to consider the potential for these policy recommendations to address the barriers to literacy confronting adults with a mental handicap.

To address what is considered to be a mounting literacy "crisis" a number of provincial and territorial governments are developing an explicit policy framework for the delivery of literacy education. In addition to concerns about the importance of literacy to economic development and a skilled labour force, governments are concerned about the "quality of life" of those without functional literacy skills; about issues of coordination given the multiplicity of government funding and program arrangements; about the significant funding allocations now being made under a variety of arrangements; and about issues of equitable access to literacy education. Development of policy recommendations is being carried out at the provincial/territorial level through the establishment of literacy task forces, departmental and interdepartmental committees, and advisory councils on literacy.

It is useful to state in general terms why an explicit policy, whether for literacy education or in other areas, is important. Five reasons can be identified. An explicit policy:

- articulates policy principles;

90

- mandates authority;
- can make provision for needed income, goods, or services;
- specifies delivery mechanisms; and,
- can establish mechanisms for collaboration with and among interest groups.

First, an explicit policy makes clear the principles and goals for which governments will allocate resources. The ways in which resources are allocated, and the impact of these allocations, can thus be judged.

Second, a policy framework designates responsibilities within government departments and ministries for making resource allocation decisions. By mandating authority to certain departments, ministries, or other bodies, governments ensure that decision-making structures are put in place to allocate resources. By mandating authority they also enable the management of accountability of government.

Third, a policy framework specifies the kinds of income, goods, and services for which governments will allocate resources. In so doing, governments make commitments for which they can be held accountable.

Fourth, a policy framework identifies the mechanisms that will be used for delivering income or goods and services. This is a critical policy choice. It determines how income, goods, or services will be provided and by whom. It also determines the decision-making procedures that will be used for their provision.

Fifth, a policy framework specifies how governments will work with various interest groups in society. It can thus grant status to certain groups to have a say in how policy and programs are to be formulated and implemented.

The proposals for a policy on literacy now being put forth in some provinces incorporate, to a greater or lesser extent, these five aspects of an explicit policy framework. Not all jurisdictions have undertaken, completed, or published a set of policy proposals for an explicit literacy policy. In the past year those that have include British Columbia, Manitoba, and Newfoundland. In British Columbia, the Provincial Literacy Advisory Committee presented its Report to the Minister of Advanced Education, Training and Technology in December, 1989. The Report was titled *Opening the Doors to Lifelong Learning: Empowering Undereducated Adults.* The Manitoba Task Force on Literacy presented its Report to theProvincial Government in April of 1989. The report was titled *Pathways for the Learner: A Strategy for Literacy for Manitobans.* In 1989, the Ministerial Advisory Committee on Literacy presented its report to the Newfoundland Minister of Education. The report was titled *Literacy in a Changing Society: Policies, Perspectives, and Strategies for Newfoundland and Labrador.* The policy recommendations presented to the provincial governments in these three provinces address to some degree the literacy issues identified throughout the provinces and terrritories. The following discussion examines the potential for these recommendations to address the kinds of barriers to literacy identified in the previous chapter. The recommendations are discussed in general terms and according to the five aspects of an explicit policy framework identified above.

First, principles related to ensuring wider access to literacy have been recommended. The Newfoundland recommendation is the strongest in this regard. The recommendation to the provincial government is that it adopt a policy statement that incorporates the principle of "literacy as a basic human right," and a goal for "universal access to programs." Principles emphasizing learner-centred literacy education that is more responsive to individuals and communities have been articulated in recommendations. All of these principles clearly address the needs of adults with a mental handicap who have experienced systematic exclusion from literacy education.

Second, recommendations in these three provinces, and literacy initiatives in other jurisdictions, identify a lead ministry that is to be explicitly mandated to implement and coordinate a literacy policy. The lack of this mandated authority has been found in some jurisdictions to hinder the implementation of a concerted strategy to address the needs for literacy.

Third, the recommendations point to a number of requirements of both individuals and providers of literacy education for "income, goods, or services." The removal of financial barriers to literacy education, as well as the disincentives in existing income support programs, has been recommended. It has also been recommended in British Columbia, for instance, that appropriate provincial ministers approach the Minister of Employment and Immigration to initiate changes to policies that discourage those on UIC from participating in literacy education. Further, it has been recommended that provincial governments request the federal government to "direct purchase" literacy education for those below the grade 7 level. Similar recommendations have been made in Newfoundland. Such policy changes would clearly address some of the barriers to literacy for adults with a mental handicap. The need for program funding, for resources for educator/tutor training and development, and for educational materials are also addressed in recommendations. All of these resources, if allocated in ways that addressed the needs of adults with a mental handcap, would remove some of the barriers they currently face.

There is a recognition in the Newfoundland and British Columbia documents that there are barriers to literacy education for adults with a disability, and that policies and programs must address their needs for support. There are few recommendations, however, that would accomplish this. In effect, the recommendations simply state a principle that the needs of adults with a disability should be addressed. The recommendation in Newfoundland is the strongest. It states: "That all literacy programmes and facilities be accessible to the disabled, including the hearing and sight impaired."

Fourth, recommendations address the need for more effective coordination between diverse delivery mechanisms whether community colleges, school boards, community-based volunteer tutor programs, or library programs. More effective coordination at the delivery level would address the need for program linkages, another barrier to literacy for adults with a mental handicap. Program linkages are required so that adults with a mental handicap can access a variety of opportunities for literacy and other education.

Fifth, recommendations point to the need for "partnerships" between government, educational and training institutions, community organizations, business, labour, and other interest groups. In Manitoba, for instance, the formation of a Manitoba Adult Literacy Council is recommended. It would include representation from a variety of interests in the area of literacy and would be mandated to support literacy activities with the community at large, in five main areas: aboriginal literacy, multicultural literacy, urban literacy, rural literacy, and northern literacy. Initiatives and recommendations in other provinces also stress the need for this kind of collaboration if literacy needs are to be effectively addressed. If adults with a disability are represented in these "partnerships" the attitudinal barriers to literacy they confront may begin to be addressed.

The policy proposals and recommendations discussed above begin to address the needs of adults with a mental handicap. However, there are a number of significant gaps in current policy recommendations.

The recognition of the needs of adults with a disability in these recommendations is critical. It should be explicitly stated, however, that policies will recognize not only the needs of those with a physical, sensory, or learning disability, —the needs of adults with a mental handicap should also be acknowledged. With the exception of Newfoundland, policy principles have not been articulated that would ensure access to the programs and facilities to which other adults have access. Initiatives to establish the required mechanisms, program standards, and guidelines are thus lacking as well. Given the systematic exclusion of adults with a mental handicap, policy recommendations that are much more proactive with regard to ensuring equality of access are required.

The need for income support has been recognized, as have the financial disincentives to participation in literacy education. However, the support needs of adults with a disability require that policies concerning provision of attendant care must also be changed. As well, if programs and facilities are to accommodate adults with a mental handicap and/or with another disability, providers of literacy education will require resources. Policies should enable providers to make these accommodations. Further, resources should be allocated so that effective training and development programs can be designed and delivered. These programs must assist educators and tutors to provide literacy education that addresses the particular needs of adults with a mental handicap. Without these resources it is likely that exclusionary eligibility criteria will be used. These criteria may seem necessary if programs do not have the resources to accommodate adults with a mental handicap and to assist them in realizing their potential to become literate.

Coordination and linkage among delivery mechanisms for literacy education has also been acknowledged as a critical need. However, because of attitudinal barriers, the existing resources for program support, counselling, and referral have impeded access to literacy education by adults with a mental handicap. Policies acknowledging their needs should also ensure that these impediments are removed.

Finally, to the extent that there is willingness, effort, and support to include self advocates, and groups who speak for adults with a mental handicap, "partnership" initiatives could contribute to community-wide awareness of issues of literacy and mental handicap. To date, recommendations in this regard have not been forthcoming. Given the significant attitudinal barriers to literacy encountered by adults with a mental handicap, such initiatives are essential.

CONCLUSION AND RECOMMENDATIONS

This report has examined the needs for literacy and for access to literacy education among adults with a mental handicap. It is estimated that a very high proportion of adults with a mental handicap have few or no literacy skills. The lack of literacy among this group is one of the obstacles to their participation and independence in the community. It has contributed to entrenching poverty, unemployment, and low health status in their lives. It has excluded them from a labour market where literacy skills are essential. And it has posed severe limitations to their enjoyment of basic human rights.

Contrary to a sometimes popular assumption, for the vast majority of adults with a mental handicap "illiteracy" is not a necessary result of their disability. This study and other research indicates that adults who have been labelled with a mental handicap have a capacity to develop literacy skills, and their exclusion from opportunities to develop these skills is one factor that explains their low levels of literacy. Many adults with a mental handicap are caught in a "vicious circle." Often the first step in acquiring literacy skills is for adults to take some control of the learning process, to have a sense of why they want literacy skills, and to be able to articulate this desire. Because of their label, and their disability, the opportunity to take control or to express autonomy in any aspect of their life is rare. As a result, the first step to literacy is not taken. When it is, it is taken slowly and with great difficulty. There are limits to the literacy skills that most adults with a mental handicap can develop. But the

96

limits to their learning currently reside less in themselves than in society as a whole.

To address the need for literacy among a large proportion of adults in Canada, the provincial/territorial and federal levels of government have made some provisions for the delivery of literacy education. This study found extensive barriers to literacy education for adults with a mental handicap: attitudinal barriers, policy and program barriers, and barriers to learning. The attitudes of many tutors, educators, program coordinators, counsellors, and other professionals stand in the way of literacy education for adults with a mental handicap. The policy framework for income support, training, and education creates some learning opportunities for adults with a mental handicap, but often excludes them from literacy education. Assessment procedures and eligibility criteria are restrictive. Supports and services used or required by an individual can also restrict access to literacy education. Program outreach to adults with a mental handicap is inadequate. Coordination of programs with other supports in individuals' lives, and with other educational and training opportunities is also inadequate for this group. Literacy programs, because of insufficient funding and insufficiently or inadequately trained educators and tutors, do not have the human resources to work with adults with a mental handicap. Program resources and materials that are accessible to adults, that provide them with useful information, and that speak to their own experiences are lacking. Finally, programs are much less responsive to individual goals and needs than they could and should be.

There are many barriers in society to learning and literacy for adults with a mental handicap. The following set of recommendations suggests ways in which barriers to literacy education could be addressed.

POLICY DEVELOPMENT

To increase access to literacy education, changes in a number of policy areas need to be considered:

- literacy policy
- policies for income support
- policies for vocational training

Literacy policy

A number of provinces are developing recommendations for provincial literacy policy. Policy analysis and recommendations have acknowledged the needs of adults with a physical disability, a learning disability, or "special needs." No explicit attention has been given to adults with a mental handicap. This is a major gap in policy. Recognition of the needs of adults with a mental handicap should be incorporated into policy formulation and recommendations.

Policy principles are being developed for provincial/ territorial literacy policy, stressing that all adults should be assured access to literacy education. However, eligibility criteria that systematically exclude adults with a mental handicap continue to be formulated and applied. These include criteria for entrance requirements, and time-limited criteria for maintaining participation in literacy education. These criteria need critical examination in light of the principles being espoused for equal access to literacy education. Exculsions from programs cannot be justified simply on the grounds that adults with a mental handicap take more time to learn, or only develop below-average levels of literacy.

There is an alternative to implementation of exclusionary criteria. Literacy policies should provide for the allocation of resources that enable programs to assist adults with a mental handicap more effectively. Resources are required for the training of educators and tutors; for the development of materials for effective community outreach to adults with a mental handicap; and for coordination and linkage with other training and education opportunities. Providers may also require resources to make accommodations to their facilities and to make needed personal

98

supports available.

To limit the use of exclusionary criteria, more stringent program standards and guidelines should be considered. Policy principles, and program standards and guidelines, should ensure that programs integrate and include adults with a disability, and not simply segregate them in other programs.

Funding of literacy education should take into account the importance of the support role of program coordinators. The research suggests that in the case of many programs more adequate support is required for educators and tutors. Without this they are less likely to feel confident in assisting adults with a mental handicap in learning literacy skills. The consequence is that fewer educators and tutors are willing to assist them.

Government initiatives to promote community awareness of literacy issues should address the literacy issues of adults with a mental handicap and adults with other disabilities. As well, government/community "partnerships" for the implementation of literacy initiatives should include representation from disability groups.

Policies for income support

Eligibility rules in the provision of social assistance and unemployment insurance have resulted in barriers and disincentives to literacy education for adults with a mental handicap.[1] There have been some efforts to remove these disincentives and to encourage training and education for social assistance recipients and UI claimants. However, increased access to literacy education by adults with a mental handicap has not resulted. One reason is that under some rules literacy education is generally excluded as a justifiable training or education option for those on social assistance or unemployment insurance. These rules need to be changed if the advantages of literacy education are to be realized. An adult's requirement for attendant care or other personal support must also be taken into account when considering the provision of income support for literacy education.

Limited access for adults with a mental handicap is also due to the wide discretionary powers of officials responsible for delivering income support. Many wrongly assume that literacy education is not a viable alternative for adults with a mental handicap. Social workers, and educational, and vocational counsellors are in a position to make recommendations about financial assistance and literacy education. They should more actively consider this option in educational and vocational assessment and counselling. This will require greater linkages with available literacy programs, and greater awareness of both the learning potential and the support needs of adults with a mental handicap in literacy education.

Policies for vocational training

There are a number of funding and program arrangements to provide pre-vocational and vocational training to adults in general and to adults with a mental handicap in particular. These arrangements by and large have excluded adults with a mental handicap from access to literacy education. Federal funding for the purchase of pre-vocational and vocational training seats excludes adults who do not achieve an academic level of grade 7 or above, the case for many adults with a mental handicap. This exclusionary criterion should be further examined. It is justified on the basis that education is a provincial responsibility. However, the use of a grade 7 achievement level seems unjustifiably arbitrary. Further, assessment tools to indicate grade level attained are unreliable.

As well, the federal government has identified individuals with a disability as one of the target groups both for employment equity legislation and for the Canadian Jobs Strategy, under which purchases of training are made. For these reasons, justifications for limiting certain adults, including most of those with a mental handicap, from obtaining literacy education must be approached with skepticism.

Training programs for adults with a mental handicap do not generally include a strong literacy component, although this is changing in some instances. Further efforts in this regard should be encouraged. Provincial officials responsible for recommending and granting training allowances, and for funding programs should also be encouraged to consider literacy education as an alternative for adults. Literacy skills can substantially widen the range of possible vocational training and employment opportunities available to individuals.

DELIVERY OF LITERACY EDUCATION

To address access issues at a program level, certain changes are necessary: changes to learner assessment procedures; to the process of training and development of educators and tutors; to outreach and linkage activities; to the kinds of materials developed; and to program responsiveness to individual need. To encourage providers of literacy programs to make these changes, the following initiatives are recommended.

Documentation of "Best Practices"

There are literacy programs that are inclusive of adults with a mental handicap. Accessible documentation about these programs is lacking. Specifically, information is required about learner assessment, training and development, accommodation of adults with a mental handciap, outreach and linkage, and methods for working with adults with a mental handicap. Documentation should be developed and widely distributed. This information is essential to enable providers of literacy education to make their programs more accessible.

Materials Development

There is a need for materials that can be used by adults with a mental handicap who participate in literacy education. Materials of two types are required in addition to what is easily produced or currently available. First, a variety of information displayed in accessible formats and written in plain language would be useful: information about health and social services, landlord and tenant issues, using legal aid, etc. Some organizations are beginning to develop these kinds of materials. Distribution to providers of literacy education should be encouraged, and production of further materials should be promoted.

Second, narratives, poetry, and other documentation about the experience of adults with a mental handicap should be produced, marketed and distributed to providers of literacy education, and the resource centres they use. These materials can be useful resources for adults with a mental handicap in literacy education. They provide a basis for an adult learner to give his or her own experience meaning. This can be an important step to literacy, one which has been found to be difficult for adults with a mental handicap. Such resources can also sensitize tutors and educators to the experiences of adult learners, to the daily issues they face, and to their potential.

Outreach
While relationships between Associations for Community Living (ACLs) and providers of literacy education are beginning to evolve, these links are minimal. Nor are links adequately developed between providers, self advocates, and People First. To further the outreach capacity of literacy programs to this community of adults these links should be encouraged. National People First, along with its provincial and local chapters, provincial ACLs, and provincial organizations for adult literacy could work together to design outreach initiatives. This collaboration should also be encouraged at the local and national levels. ACLs and People First may also be able to provide resources to be used in awareness training of educators and tutors. (The Appendix provides a contact list of these organizations).

Linkages
The barriers that adults with a mental handicap encounter to literacy education are also found in other educational opportunities whether adult basic education, academic upgrading, prevocational, or vocational training. For two reasons, more and more adults with a mental handicap are likely to encounter barriers to the education and training system. First, as the barriers to literacy education are addressed for this group of adults, they are likely to seek further educational opportunities. Second, as an increasing number of individuals with a mental handicap progress through the regular school system, they are likely to look toward the community college system and university for further education. Policy and program development should anticipate these trends. Counselling, information, and funding assistance that enables linkages between these various sets of programs should be encouraged.

Program Evaluation

Evaluation of literacy education should be designed to incorporate criteria for assessing accessibility by adults with a mental handicap. Criteria related to the various factors affecting access (discussed in Chapter 6) should be incorporated. Thus, evaluations should examine procedures for admitting individuals into literacy education, training and development strategies, outreach initiatives, availability of materials, responsiveness to individual needs, reasonable accommodation of individuals' needs for support, etc.

RESEARCH

We know less about the actual levels of literacy among adults with a mental handicap than about many other groups of adults in the population. This is because surveys of disability and surveys of literacy have not been integrated. Future national surveys of disability should be designed to incorporate a set of items to test literacy levels among this group. The set of test items used by Statistics Canada in the recent national literacy survey could be used or adapted. Alternatively, literacy surveys could be stratified to include a sample of adults with a mental handicap. The numbers of adults surveyed, however, would not likely constitute a sample from which valid estimates could be made of the scale of the problem. In either case, data collected would provide some standard against which to analyze trends in the future. It would also provide a basis on which to examine the factors that contribute to or pose barriers to literacy for this group.

Some capacity to generate data on the numbers of adults with a disability currently involved in literacy education, other adult basic education programs, and academic upgrading is also required. This capacity is necessary to begin an analysis of trends and to assess the impact of literacy policies on access to literacy education by adults with a disability.

Notes

[1]For a general discussion of how eligibility rules in social assistance and income-in-kind programs pose disincentives and barriers to individuals with a disability see Sherri Torjman, *Income Insecurity;* The G. Allan Roeher Institute, *Poor Places* (Toronto: 1990).

References

Adult Literacy and Basic Skills Unit (February 1982). *Literacy and Numeracy Work with Mentally Handicapped Adults.* London.

Alberta. Northern Alberta Development Council (March 1989). *Adult Literacy in Northern Alberta: A Background Report.* Edmonton.

Alderson-Gill & Associates Consulting Inc. (June 1989). *Study of Literacy and Learning Disabilities.* Ottawa: Learning Disabilities Association of Canada.

Arctic College, North West Territories (1990). *Arctic College Strategic Plan.* Yellowknife.

Barry, B. (1989). *Spreading the Word: A Handbook for Setting Up a Community-Based Literacy Program.* St. John's: Newfoundland and Labrador Association of Youth Serving Agencies.

Bataille, L. (Ed.). (1975.) *A Turning Point for Literacy,* Proceedings of the International Symposium for Literacy, Persepolis, Iran, September 3-8, 1975. New York: Pergamon Press.

Blanton, L.P., Semmel, M.I. & Rhodes, S.S. (1987). Research on the reading of mildly mentally retarded learners: a synthesis of the empirical literature. In Sheldon Rosenberg (Ed.), *Advances in applied psycholinguistics, Volume 2: Reading, writing and language learning.* Cambridge: Cambridge University Press.

Bray, N. W. & Turner, L. A. (1987). Production Anomalies (Not Strategic Deficiencies) in Mentally Retarded Individuals. *Intelligence,* 11, 49-60.

British Columbia. Provincial Literacy Advisory Committee (December 1989). *Opening the Doors to Lifelong Learning: Empowering Undereducated Adults*. Victoria: Ministry of Advanced Education, Training, and Technology.

Brown, H. D. (1980). *Principles of Language Learning and Teaching*. Englewood Cliffs, N.J.: Prentice Hall.

Cairns, J. C. (February 1988). *Adult Illiteracy in Canada*. Toronto: Council of Ministers of Education.

Campione, J.C. (1987). Metacognitive components of instructional research with problem learners. In F.E. Weinert and R.H. Kluwe Eds.), *Metacognition, motivation, and understanding*. Hillsdale, New Jersy: Lawrence Erlbaum Associates.

Campione, J.C. & Brown, A.L. (1977). Memory and metamemory development in educable retarded children. In R.V. Kail and J.W. Hagen Eds.), *Perspectives on the development of memory and cognition*. Hillsdale, N.J.: Lawrence Erlbaum Associates.

Canada. Employment and Immigration Canada formerly Department of Manpower and Immigration. *Annual Reports* (dating from 1970/71). Ottawa.

Canada. Employment and Immigration Canada (April 1989). *Success in the Works: A Policy Paper. A Labour Force Development Strategy for Canada*. Ottawa.

Canada. Health and Welfare Canada (1986). *Achieving Health for All*. Ottawa: National Health and Welfare.

Canada. Health and Welfare Canada (1989). *Charting Canada's Future: A Report of the Demographic Review*. Ottawa.

Canada. Statistics Canada (March 1990). *The Health and Activity Limitation Survey Highlights: Disabled Persons in Canada*. Ottawa.

Canada. Statistics Canada June (1988). *The Health and Activity Limitation Survey User's Guide*. Ottawa.

Canada. Statistics Canada (1990). *Survey of Literacy Skills Used in Daily Activities: Survey Overview*. Ottawa.

Carpenter, T. (1986). *The Right to Read: Tutor's Handbook for SCIL Program: Student Centred Individualized Learning.* Toronto: Frontier College Press.

Creative Research Group (1987). *Literacy in Canada: A research report.* Ottawa: Southam News.

Daina A. Bruners and Associates (March 1989). *Fairview College's Northern Region Adult Literacy Program: The Impact of Literacy on the Lives of Students and Tutors.* Edmonton: Northern Alberta Development Council.

Doré, L. (1982). *Des gens comme vous et moi.* Montréal: Editions coopératives St. Martin.

Doré, L. (October 1986). On n'apprend pas à nager dans un bain. *Alpha Liaison*, 71), 19-22.

Fletcher, D. & Abood, D. (September 1988). An Analysis of the Readability of Product Warning Labels: Implications for Curriculum Development for Persons with Moderate and Severe Mental Retardation. *Education and Training in Mental Retardation.* 23(3) 224-227.

Forest, M. & Kappel, B. (1988). *It's About Learning: A Student Centred Approach to Adult Learning.* Toronto: Frontier College Press.

Freedman, J. (1988). *The Accessibility of Literacy Upgrading in the Community for Adults with Disabilities.* Toronto: Centre for Independent Living in Toronto.

Freire, P. (1970). *Pedagogy of the Oppressed.* New York: The Seabury Press.

Freire, P. & Macedo, D. (1987). *Literacy: Reading the Word and the World.* South Hadley, Mass.: Bergin and Harvey Publishers.

Frontier College & the Ontario Public Health Association (1989). *Literacy and Health: Phase I, Making the World Healthier and Safer for People who Can't Read.* Toronto: Ontario Public Health Association.

108

Gottlieb, B.W. (1982). Social facilitation influences on the oral reading performance of academically handicapped children. *American Journal of Mental Deficiency*, 87, 153-158.

Gower, D. (April 1988). *Labour market activity of disabled persons in Canada*. Ottawa: Statistics Canada.

Gray, W.S. (1956). *The Teaching of Reading and Writing: An Instructional Survey*. Paris: UNESCO.

Hamilton, M. K. (1989). The Health and Activity Limitation Survey. In Statistics Canada, *Health Reports*, (12).

Harman, D. (1987). *Illiteracy: A National Dilemma*. New York: Cambridge Book Company.

Hunter, C. & Harman, D. (1979). *Adult Illiteracy in the United States: A Report to the Ford Foundation*. New York: McGraw-Hill.

International Council for Adult Education (1988). Literacy and Disabled Persons: Don't Label Us as Problems. In Margaret Gayfer (Ed.), *Literacy in Industrialized Countries: A Focus on Practice*, Report of workshop proceedings. Toronto.

Johnston, P. H. (1985). Understanding Reading Disability: A Case Study Approach. *Harvard Educational Review*, 55(2), 153-177.

Karassik, J. W. (1989). *Literacy and Learning Disabilities: A handbook for literacy workers*. Ottawa: Learning Disabilities Association of Canada.

Katims, D. S. & Alexander, R. N. (1987). Cognitive Strategy Training: Implications, Applications, Limitations. (Paper presented at the annual convention of the Council for Exceptional Children, Chicago, April 20-24).

Levine, K. (August 1982). Functional Literacy: Fond Illusions and False Economies. *Harvard Educational Review*, 52(3), 249-266.

Levine, K. (1986). *The Social Context of Literacy*. London: Routledge and Kegan Paul.

Lewis, M. & Simon, R. (1986). A Discourse Not Intended for Her: Learning and Teaching within Patriarchy. *Harvard Educational Review*, 56, 457-472.

Lytle, Su. (Fall 1988). From the Inside Out: Reinventing Assessment. *Focus on Basics,* 2(1).

Kozol, J. (1985). *Illiterate America.* New York: Doubleday.

Manitoba. Manitoba Task Force on Literacy April 1989. *Pathways for the Learner: A Strategy for Literacy for Manitobans.* Winnipeg.

Martin, J. E. & Mithaug, D. (1986). Advancing a Technology of Self-Control. *B.C. Journal of Special Education,* 10(2), 93-99.

McLaren, P. (May 1988). Culture or Canon? Critical Pedagogy and the Politics of Literacy. *Harvard Educational Review*, 58(2), 213-234.

Metropolitan Toronto Association for Community Living Spring 1990. *Profile.* Toronto.

Miller, A. (1987). *Improving Educational Opportunities for Disabled Adults Through Open Learning.* Richmond, British Columbia: Open Learning Institute.

Monteith, L. (1989). The Integrated Approach: A Vision for Adult Literacy in the Toronto Board in the 1990s. Toronto: Adult Basic Education Unit, Toronto Board of Education.

Morrice, D. (July 27, 1989), "In the courtroom, disability means more than ramps and wheelchairs." *The Globe and Mail.*

Newfoundland. Ministerial Advisory Committee on Literacy (1989). *Literacy in a Changing Society: Policies, Perspectives, and Strategies for Newfoundland and Labrador.* St. John's: Department of Education.

Newfoundland. Royal Commission on Employment and Unemployment (1985). *Education for Self-Reliance.* Education Report of the Royal Commission on Employment and Unemployment. St. John's.Author.

110

Ontario. Ministry of Skills Development (1988). *A Directory of Literacy and Adult Basic Education Programs in Ontario.* Toronto.

Oxenham, J. (1980). *Literacy: Writing, reading and social organization.* London: Routledge and Kegan Paul.

Patton, J. R. & Polloway, E. A. (1988). Curriculum Orientations. In Greg A. Robinson Ed.), *Best Practices in Mental Disabilities. Volume 2.* (ERIC Document Reproduction Service No. ED 304 830).

Québec. Commission d'étude sur la formation des adultes (Commission Jean) (1982). *Apprendre: une action volontaire et responsable.* Québec: Ministère des communications.

Rawls, J. (1971). *A Theory of Justice.* Cambridge, Mass.: Harvard University Press.

Rioux, M. (1989). *Last in the Queue* (Occasional Paper). Toronto: The G. Allan Roeher Institute.

Rockhill, K. (1987). "Gender, Language and the Politics of Literacy." *British Journal of Sociology of Education,* 8, 153-167.

Saskatchewan. Department of Education (February 1988). *Removing Barriers: Accessibility to Adult Basic Education for Disabled Adults.* Regina.

Scottish Community Education Council (1987). *Moving Ahead: A new handbook for tutors helping mentally handicapped adults to learn.* Edinburgh, Scotland.

Senn, C. (1988). *Vulnerable: Sexual Abuse and People with an Intellectual Handicap.* Toronto: The G. Allan Roeher Institute.

The G. Allan Roeher Institute (1988). *Income Insecurity: The Disability Income System in Canada.* Toronto.

The G. Allan Roeher Institute (1990). *Poor Places: Disability-Related Residential and Support Services.* Toronto.

Shapiro, E. (1981). Self-control procedures with the mentally retarded. In M. Hersen, R. Eisler & P. Miller (Eds.), *Progress in behaviour modification,* vol. 12. New York: Academic Press.

Sola, M. & Bennett, A. T. (1985). The Struggle for Voice: Literacy and Consciousness in an East Harlem School. *Journal of Education*, 167, 88-110.

Stevens, E. W. Jr. (1988). *Literacy, Law, and Social Order*. DeKalb, Illinois: Northern Illinois University Press.

Toronto Board of Education (October 1985). *The Right to Learn*. Toronto.

Turner, J. E. (1987). Social Influences on Cognitive Strategies and Cognitive Development: The Role of Communication and Instruction. *Intelligence*, 11.

TVOntario (1989). *Lifeline to Literacy: People with Disabilities Speak Out*. Toronto: The Ontario Education Communications Authority.

Whitman, T. L. (1990). Self-Regulation and Mental Retardation. *American Journal on Mental Retardation*, 9(44), 347-362.

Willinsky, J. (1990). The Construction of a Crisis: Literacy in Canada. *Canadian Journal of Education*, 1(51), 1-15.

Woods Gordon Management Consultants (October 1987). *The Cost of Illiteracy to Business in Canada*. For the Canadian Business Task Force on Literacy. Toronto: Canadian Business Task Force on Literacy.

APPENDIX A

List of Contacts:

Provincial/Territorial Literacy Organizations

Literacy B.C.
c/o Invergarry Learning Centre
14525 - 110A Avenue
Surrey, British Columbia
V3R 2B4
tel: (604) 584-5424

Yukon Literacy Council
206A Hanson Street
Whitehorse, Yukon
Y1A 1Y4
tel: (403) 668-6280

Alberta Association for Adult Literacy
Box 425
Edmonton, Alberta
T5J 2K1
tel: (403) 320-3388
    (403) 329-7283

N.W.T. Literacy Council
Box 8
Iqaluit, North West Territories
X0A 0H0
tel: (819) 979-4376

Saskatchewan Literacy Network
c/o Saskatchewan Institute for Applied
 Science and Technology
P.O. Box 1520
Saskatoon, Saskatchewan
S7K 3R5
tel:(306) 933-7368

Literacy Worker's Alliance of Manitoba
304 - 414 Graham Avenue
Winnipeg, Manitoba
R3C 0L8
tel:(204) 943-1170
    (204) 943-1180

Ontario Literacy Coalition
365 Bloor St. East, Suite 1003
Toronto, Ontario
M4W 3M7
tel:(416) 963-5787

Regroupement des groupes francophones
d'alphabétisation populaire de l'Ontario
555 Bloor St. West
Toronto, Ontario
M5S 1Y6

Regroupement des groupes populaires en
alphabétisation du Québec Inc.
App. #1, 5040, boulevard St-Laurent
Montréal (Québec)
H2T 1R7
tel:(514) 277-9976

New Brunswick Committee on Literacy
c/o Saint John Human Development Council
Box 6125, Station A
City Market Building
47 Charlotte St., 3rd Floor
Saint John, New Brunswick
E2L 4R6
tel:(506) 634-1673

Fédération d'alphabétisation du N.B. Inc.
C.P. 459
Richibouctou (Nouveau Brunswick)
E0A 2M0
tel: (506) 523-7660

Provincial Literacy Volunteers
P.O. Box 400
Charlottetown, P.E.I.
C1A 7K7
tel: (902) 368-3620

Comité Consultatif provincial pour
l'alphabétisation de l'I.P.E.
340 Court Street
P.O. Box 1330
Summerside, P.E.I.
tel: (902) 436-4881

Newfoundland and Labrador Literacy Coalitions
Suite 118
15 Rowan Street
St. John's, Newfoundland
A1A 2X2

OR
Bill Barry
4A Lower Battery Road
St. John's, Newfoundland A1A 1A1
tel: (709) 576-1412

Provincial/Territorial Associations for Community Living

British Columbia Association for
Community Living
300 - 30 East 6th Avenue
Vancouver, B.C.
V5T 4P4
tel: (604) 875-1119

Alberta Association for Community Living
11728 Kingsway Avenue
Edmonton, Alberta
T5G 0X5
tel: (403) 451-3055

Saskatchewan Association for Community Living
3031 Louise Street
Saskatoon, Saskatchewan
S7J 3L1
tel: (306) 955-3344

Association for Community Living - Manitoba
1 - 90 Market Avenue
Winnipeg, Manitoba
R3B 0P3
tel: (204) 947-1118

Ontario Association for Community Living
180 Duncan Mill Road, Suite 600
Don Mills, Ontario
M3B 1Z6
tel: (416) 447-4348

Association du Québec pour l'intégration sociale
3958 Dandurand
Montréal (Québec)
H1X 1P7
tel: (514) 725-7245

Canadian Association for Community Living -
Nova Scotia Division
83 Portland Street
Dartmouth, Nova Scotia
B2Y 1H5
tel: (902) 469-1174

New Brunswick Association for Community Living
86 York Street, 2nd Floor
Fredericton, New Brunswick
E3B 3N5
tel: (506) 458-8866

Prince Edward Island Association for Community Living
P.O. Box 280
Charlottetown, P.E.I.
C1A 7K5
tel: (902) 566-4844

Newfoundland Association for Community Living
P. O. Box 5453
St. John's, Newfoundland
A1C 5W4
tel: (709) 722-0790

Yukon Association for Community Living
P.O. Box 4853
Whitehorse, Yukon
Y1A 4N6
tel: (403) 667-4606

Yellowknife Association for Community Living
P.O. Box 981
Yellowknife, Northwest Territories
X1A 2N7
tel: (403) 920-2644

National People First

National People First Project
Kinsmen Building, York University Campus
4700 Keele Street
Downsview, Ontario
M3J 1P3
tel: (416) 661-9611

For provincial and local chapters of People First contact the National office, 4700 Keele Street, 2nd Floor.

Selected Publications of The G. Allan Roeher Institute

entourage is a quarterly bilingual magazine that looks at how people with mental handicaps can be supported *by* the community to live, learn, work, and have fun *in* the community. *entourage* includes the most current information on issues and upcoming events, and provides the most comprehensive way of keeping in touch with what's happening in the lives of individuals with a mental handicap.

Subscriptions: $18 Canadian $20 foreign (1 year)
                    $32 Canadian $36 foreign (2 years)
                    $48 Canadian $52 foreign (3 years)

The Language of Pain: Perspectives on Challenging Behaviour, 1988

Community Living 2000, 1987

Income Insecurity: The Disability Income System in Canada, 1988

Righting Wrongs: Disability, Your Ombudsperson and You, 1989

Poor Places: Disability-Related Residential and Support Services, 1990

Vulnerable: Sexual Abuse and People With An Intellectual Handicap, 1988

Making Friends: Developing Relationships Between People With Disabilities and Other Members Of The Community, 1990

Service Brokerage: Individual Empowerment and Social service accountability, 1990

Literacy and Labels: A Look at Literacy Policy and People With Mental Handicaps, 1990

The Power to Choose: An Examination of Service Brokerage and Individualized Funding as Implemented by the Community Living Society, 1990

For more information, please contact:

The G. Allan Roeher Institute
Kinsmen Building, York University Campus
4700 Keele Street, Downsview, Ontario M3J 1P3
Telephone: (416) 661-9611
Fax: (416) 661-5701